YOUR KNOWLEDGE

- We will publish your bachelor's and
  master's thesis, essays and papers

- Your own eBook and book -
  sold worldwide in all relevant shops

- Earn money with each sale

Upload your text at www.GRIN.com
and publish for free

Bibliographic information published by the German National Library:

The German National Library lists this publication in the National Bibliography; detailed bibliographic data are available on the Internet at http://dnb.dnb.de .

Imprint:

Copyright © 2009 GRIN Verlag, Open Publishing GmbH
Print and binding: Books on Demand GmbH, Norderstedt Germany
ISBN: 9783640518302

This book at GRIN:

http://www.grin.com/en/e-book/141994/the-functional-actor-in-the-securitization-process

Ricarda Popa

The Functional Actor in the Securitization Process

What Social – Psychological Requirements of the Functional Actor Facilitate Securitization, According to the Social Identity Theory and the Social Balance Theory?

GRIN Publishing

GRIN - Your knowledge has value

Since its foundation in 1998, GRIN has specialized in publishing academic texts by students, college teachers and other academics as e-book and printed book. The website www.grin.com is an ideal platform for presenting term papers, final papers, scientific essays, dissertations and specialist books.

Visit us on the internet:

http://www.grin.com/

http://www.facebook.com/grincom

http://www.twitter.com/grin_com

What Social – Psychological Requirements of the Functional Actor Facilitate Securitization, According to the Social Identity Theory and the Social Balance Theory?

Research Paper

In the field of Peace and Conflict Studies

at the
Faculty of Social Science and Philosophy
at the Philipps University in Marburg

Elaborated by

Ramona Ricarda Popa

Marburg, March 2009

What Social – Psychological Requirements of the Functional Actor Facilitate Securitization, According to the Social Identity Theory and the Social Balance Theory?

Table of contents

Introduction

The aim of this research paper is to ascertain, by means of the Social Identity Theory, the social psychological characteristics that facilitate the occurrence of the securitizing act on behalf of the actor of the Copenhagen School"s Securitization Theory, termed as functional actor, and more commonly known as ‚significant addressed audience"1, in order to understand what are the factors that determine it to consent to securitization, since this category of actor has been left untheorized, despite of its key role in the securitization process.

The departure point is a question that the authors of the securitization theory, themselves address: "When does an argument [...] achieve sufficient effect to make an audience tolerate violations of rules that would otherwise have to be obeyed? [...] For individuals and groups to speak security does not guarantee success" as "securitization is not decided by the securitizer, but by the audience of the speech act." (Buzan 1998:25,31) The only stipulation refers to the functional actor"s power to materialize securitization, being neither the referent object, nor the securitizing actor. The deficiency of theorization has impelled a social psychological elaboration of the functional actor"s distinguishing features that causes it to accept the securitizing act, since the absence of details in this respect leaves much space for interpretation, and leads to the investment of resources, when securitization analysis should not be centered upon the establishment of the actors, but upon the process and dynamics of securitization, according to the same author.

There are several assumptions from which this research paper starts: it could be easier anticipated whether the securitizing move would succeed or be impeded if there were a clearer delineation of those features of the chosen functional actor that facilitate securitization. Likewise, by the portrayal of the functional actors the theory would become more easily applicable in the security analysis, as it would help to easier determine who classifies as a significant addressed audience, before the completion of the securitizing move, since I interpret securitizing acts as those events in which the situational identity of the audience echoes its core social identity and its short term (group) identity, but also a part of its history. Accordingly, this could facilitate political decisions.

I consider *the Social Identity Theory* as the most appropriate theoretical approach in defining the functional actor, since the two theories display an evident complementarity. The social identity theory discerns the conditions in which individuals choose their ways of conduct in inter-group conflicting relations, in order to achieve a positive and higher appreciated position, while for the Copenhagen School "security is an area of competing actors". (Buzan 1998:37) Both theories centre on „powerful" inter-group processes, without ignoring the individual, the mobile for acting

---

[1] This actor will be termed in this paper „functional actor".

being identity, which must be dealt with immediately, and with all existing efforts. (Buzan 1997:24) Both consider identity evolving according to internal and external developments, and that it is subject to challenges because it is in its nature to yearn for survival and a positive appraisal. Both theories consider the individuals and their behavior as dominated by their apprehension of the social environment. "In a securitization situation, a unit [...] relies on its own resources demanding the right to govern its actions by its own priorities" (Buzan 1998:26) whereas the social identity theory may explain the functional actor, seeing that it "translates social categories into human groups, in creating a psychological reality from a social one, [...] it explores the psychological processes [...] examines the group in the individual" and defines the self-concept as it derives from the social identities (group memberships), and the behavior as group behavior, since without the group, the individual fades[2]. (Hogg 1988:17) Thus, I consider that the social identity theory reaches beyond the securitization theory and can explain the processes which make it possible that the functional actor agrees with the securitizing actor, revealing preparedness to remain in the „affected" or threatened group rather than to exchange it.

In addition to that, I shall employ Heider"s *Social Balance Theory*, which explains the interrelation of individuals and their adherence and behavior related to his environment, as the positions of the actors in the securitization theory are outlined generically, whereas "the way to study securitization is to study [...] constellations [...] and we, in security complex analysis need to find the main patterns of interaction." (Buzan 1998:25,45) The balance theory explains relatively precisely how individuals construct their relations with other individuals and objects, so as to achieve psychological balance. Akin to the securitization theory, Heider refers only indirectly to the objective reality which affects the representations, and focuses more on the representations in an individual"s life space. (Heider 1959:213) Besides that, it seizes subtle social psychological processes in clean and simple formulations that can easily be proven by facts and by statistical data. Its application on the securitization constellation can reflect the relatedness of the functional actor to the others, and indicate uncomplicatedly the reasons why the functional actor chooses the direct conflict in order to protect its identity.

As the paper embraces a theoretical pluralism, the research methodology I shall employ is a connective and integrative theoretical analysis of the above mentioned approaches. I shall employ Heider"s Balance Theory in order to schematize optically the actors" constellation, and to define the place of the functional actor in the „relations-network". Thus, I shall set up a frame within which I shall apply the propositions of the social identity theory. I shall try to integrate the social identity arguments in the explanation of the functional actor in its dyadic relations to the other actors - respectively the securitizing actor and the threat actor, deriving its features from the in-

---

[2] The membership to groups is the source of social identity. (Brown 2000:xvii)

group and inter-group processes. The prerequisite for the analysis are: the fulfillment of felicitous conditions of the securitizing move, time and space proximity of the threat, and most important, the functional actor"s consent to the securitizing act, since I will focus upon those functional actors that accept securitization, because Buzan claims that a security analysis is interested in those security events that succeed.

I shall base the paper on primary and secondary source analyses. The primary source analysis focuses on the theory of the Copenhagen School, on its quintessence and its shortcomings regarding the delineation of its actors. Likewise, the Social Identity Theory and the Social Balance Theory represent primary sources, as they bring the explaining arguments. The secondary source analysis refers to diverse studies, essays and analytical thoughts of other scholars to both the theories, for the development of critical standpoints regarding the securitization theory, these pertain among others to: *Dominic Abrams* - director of the Centre for the Study of Group Processes at the University of Kent; *Michael Hogg* - professor of Social Psychology at Claremont Graduate University, whose research focuses on group processes, intergroup relations and the self concept, and is closely associated with social identity theory; *Karina Korostelina* – research professor of conflict analysis and resolution; *Paul Roe* - researcher at the Copenhagen Peace Research Institute; *Ralf Emmers* - Deputy Head of Studies at the Institute of Defence and Strategic Studies, Singapore, but also other well-known names.

Despite of the elaboration of the functional actor from a different theoretical perspective, this paper does not claim to enlarge the securitization theory but only to work upon some aspects in order to make the theory easier applicable empirically, so that the grasping the securitizing move becomes more easily foreseeable. It does not have the claim to improve the degree of employment of the theory on countries with totalitarian regimes, where the issue to be secured often falls together with the securitizer, and political decisions with security relevance are not subject to „public" agreement; or in regions of the world, where politics is driven rather by realistic calculations than by social psychological ones (i.e. North East Asia). In like manner, the social identity theory cannot help to establish when the crossing of the border from a high politicization to securitization occurs in societies with emergent democracies.

The paper is structured on three chapters. The 1st chapter is dedicated to the theoretical frame, comprising short presentations of the securitization theory, the social identity, and the balance theory. The latter ones shall be termed „auxiliary theories" because they help the explanation of the securitization theory on another level. The 2nd chapter represents the core of the research activity, comprising the determination of the functional actor in accordance to the established variables and conditions. The 3rd chapter contains the critique to the limits of the social identity theory in answering the research question.

1. Theoretical frame

1.1 The Securitization Theory

The securitization theory developed in the late '90"s by the Copenhagen School *(Security: A New Framework for Analysis, 1998)* pertains to the latest security theories within the field of international relations. It distinguishes itself from other security theories in several aspects: first, it has widened the concept of security, which subsequently would not be characteristic only to the military sector but also to the political, economical, societal and environmental spheres. Second, it has "developed a substantial body of concepts to rethink security, most notably through its notions of *securitization* and *desecuritization* [...]," which do not pertain exclusively to the state, but can be enacted by other for as well (Buzan 1998:24), providing a framework to analyze security, namely to understand how an issue becomes securitized or desecuritized. (Emmers 2007:110) Third, it has introduced a subjective approach to security analysis, turning security into a self-referential practice on the claim that security is not an objective existing reality but an inter-subjective[3] one, being the result of social[4], subjective[5], discursive[6] processes and determined by actors with political potential, that benefit from privileged positions[7]. (Emmers 2007:112)

According to the securitization theory, an issue can be *non-politicized, politicized, securitized* or *desecuritized*. It is *non-politicized* when the specific issue is not included in the public debate; it turns *politicized* when it is dealt with in the standard political procedure; it is *securitized* when a change within the usual working manner of entities within the state takes place and there are introduced measures beyond the standard political operating procedure[8]; "securitization can be seen as a more extreme version of politicization", which "is not fulfilled only by breaking the rules, nor solely by existential threats, but by cases of existential threats that legitimize the breaking of rules." (Buzan 1998:23,25) An issue is *desecuritized* when the state of emergency is reversed to the political routine by "shifting of issues out of emergency mode and into normal bargaining processes of the political sphere". (Buzan 1998:4) Desecuritization represents "the optimal long range option since it means not to have issues phrased as threats against which we have no countermeasures". (Buzan 1998:29)

---

[3] By the reaction of the audience to the security speech act. . "Security ultimately rests neither with the objects, nor with the subjects, but *among* the subjects (Buzan 1998:31) and is established inter-subjectively. (Buzan 1998:25)
[4] Buzan 1998:31. By the interaction and coexistence of environments, values and power, some issue gain superior significance and strong political effect.
[5] By the perception of a threat by actors, who construct their threat perception in a discourse that they transmit to other involved actors.
[6] By the speech act they address to the audience.
[7] By those who have the power to decide whether to deal with an issue as a security issue.
[8] The theory does not provide for a definition of extraordinary measures.

Securitization is a 3 step process: it begins with the identification and the presentation of the threat in a rhetoric of existential threat; it continues with the request of emergency of extraordinary measures beyond the normal politics, since if the issue in question is not dealt with immediately and with all existing efforts, „everything else will be irrelevant (because we will not be here or will not be free to deal with it in our way)". (Buzan 1997:24) The securitization process completes with "the effect on their inter-unit relations by breaking free of rules" (Buzan 1998:6), namely the acceptance on behalf of the concerned that the issue is an existential threat.

As securitization is not an act pertaining exclusively to the state, the actor to raise the awareness of the security meaning of the threat by the security rhetoric is known to be the *securitizing* actor (also: securitizer), and can be political leaders, governments, bureaucracies, trade unions, popular movements, pressure groups, lobbyists, etc. (Buzan 1998:40) Its security speech act is called *securitizing move* and is addressed to an audience considered significant, termed *significant addressed audience or functional actor*. In the securitizing move, the securitizing actor declares a referent object to be existentially threatened, and frames the issue either as a special kind of politics or as above politics, calling accordingly for "politics beyond the established rules of the game. (Buzan 1998:23) The *referent object* is something with a legitimate claim to survival, *i.e.* an essential value related to the functional actor, the state, the national sovereignty, the national economy, the environment, the collective identity, individuals, an ideology, etc. *The functional actor* is usually established constitutionally, being the parliament, the junta, a crisis committee, the president/dictator, etc (Gromes/Bonacker 2007:7), but can be also the public opinion, politicians, officers, elites from various sectors, etc. It recognizes the security speech, and by its interpretation as having security meaning it can authorize and initiate extraordinary measures known as securitizing acts. If the functional actor accepts the reality of the threat to the referent object as illustrated in the securitizing move, and expresses it consent to the instauration of the state of emergency and to the initiation of extraordinary measures, than a *securitizing act* takes place. If the consent does not exist, "we can talk only of a securitizing move, not of an object actually being securitized". Thus the *securitizing act* represents the legitimate consequence of the consent to the *securitizing move*. (Buzan 1998:24-31)

In order to obtain securitization, it does not suffice that the securitizing actor presents an issue as a matter of survival, employing rhetoric of the threat, for it does not have the power to turn its securitizing move into a securitization act, but only to place it high on the security agenda. Likewise, securitization cannot be achieved only by breaking the rules. (Buzan 1998:25) To complete the securitization process, the securitizer needs the free consent of the functional actor, inasmuch as „the security act is negotiated between the securitizing agent and the audience", (Buzan 1998:26) and securitization is a phenomenon that is decided upon by the two. (Buzan

1998:32,33,40) „The functional actor (without being the referent object, or the actor calling for security on behalf of the referent object)... is an actor who significantly influences the decisions in the field of security", holding a key position in the entire process, (Buzan 1998:36) as it legitimizes actions with consequences on the idea of the state[9]. In accordance to this, the reaction sequence performed by the functional actor is deeply related to the securitizing move and cannot be treated as an independent episode.

The specificity and likewise shortcoming of the securitization theory is that it ignores the objective existing reality of the threat and focuses on the securitizing actor's subjective recording of the threat in his speech act, considering „the utterance as the primary reality" (Buzan 1997:55), after John Austin's speech act doctrine: „saying is doing". Thus, it centers on the illocution[10], ignoring the perlocution [11] , examining the conversational stratagem in „raising a new extraordinary – negative - agenda of politics and security", but not its effects. Because of this, the securitization analytical tool impairs the employment of the theory in prospective direction, being applicable successfully only retrospectively, as securitization takes place just with the occurrence of the securitization act, otherwise the analysis would not cover the entire securitization phenomenon. With this, the theory reaches its limit.[12]

Nonetheless, since the Copenhagen School has a constructivist approach to security, to cover the entire affair by regarding only the securitizing move, it may be expedient to surpass the limits of the illocution (securitizing move), by paying attention to the social psychological characteristics of the audience, in the existing actors' constellation, and see what is that which facilitates or predicts perlocution (securitizing act). This could help the analyst understand the „processes of constructing a shared understanding of what is to be collectively responded to as a threat" (Buzan 1998:26) and support him/her in making more precise predictions about the chances for a securitization act to occur, since "security analysis is interested mainly in the successful instances of securitization – the cases in which other people follow the securitizing lead, creating a social, inter-subjective constitution of a referent object on a mass scale." (Buzan 1998:39)

---

[9] That is to say to the physical base and the institutions of the state. The physical base is represented, among others, by the nation/people, the territory, the natural resources, etc. The threat to nation is thus to be seen as a threat to identity, whereas the threat to the state's institutions (?) as a threat to sovereignty. (See Buzan, 1991, Chapter 2)
[10] Illocution is the term employed by Austin when referring to express what the speaker does *in* saying something.
[11] Perlocution expresses what is done by saying something.
[12] Worthy of mentioning is that Austin himself focuses only on the speaker within the speech act, neglecting the addressee. Being a discourse and speech act theory based of Austin's principles, it is obvious that the securitization theory also leaves out this key element in the conversation, focusing only on the manner of provoking a securitizing act but not on the act itself.

1.2. 'Auxiliary Theories'

The potential of the two chosen theories in explaining the functional actor relies in their seizing it in the processes of internal organization while being confronted with the foe, and reflects its behavior as voluntary or self-regulating, being molded in accordance to its internal motivations that is the functional actor"s attitudes and beliefs. (Hogg 2001:153) The social identity theory illustrates the functional actor"s social awareness and its engagement to social acting, based on social psychological determinants of action, as it connects the individual, collective and relational elements of self. On the other hand, the social balance theory reflects the social psychological mechanisms that proceed when organising the social environment dichotomously, incorporating the 4 classical processes of the social identity theory in a more schematic way. The two theories support the other"s arguments in the sense that the social identity offers a more detailed explanation of the causal factors of the social balance"s adversary and alliance attitudes.

The two theories support the operationalization of the functional actor in the sense that, in my opinion, there are usually two kinds of functional actors: „social-political ones" (formal, institutional) and „social psychological ones"(informal, non-institutional) which may fall together, the first having the political competence of legitimizing extraordinary measures, the latter having the moral competence, and the capacity of exerting also a moral pressure, next to the legitimization of action. Whereas the first represents the „official" organization for the promoting of the latter"s interest and differ from a sector to another, the latter stays the same, in the sense that it manifests constant characteristics in relation to its environment (referent object, securitizing actor, threat actor), being identifiable on the basis of these. To this extent, according to the two above-mentioned theories, the „social psychological functional actor" is that actor, which, sharing the understanding of what is the meaning of the referent object, and what a security issue is, and being convinced that extraordinary measures presented by the securitizer are necessary, legitimizes them, having a strong internal and psychological connection with the referent object, manifesting readiness to join the securitizer for defending the referent object out of internal motivation and opposing the threat actor directly proportional with the subjective significance of the referent object for the functional actor, the two emerging blocks (functional actor/securitizer versus threat actor) excluding each other.

1.2.1 Henri Tajfel's and John Turner's Social Identity Theory

The social identity theory (SIT) is a psychological theory about the intergroup relations, group processes and the social self.[13] Together with the self-categorization theory, the stimulus classification theory and the minimal group studies, SIT forms the Social Identity Approach. (Zick 2008:413) Social identity is an open, dynamic, permanently changing system that exceeds the self and determines the relationship with the environment. It functions for the individual in various manners, reflecting its pursuit of self-esteem, increasing social status, personal safety, support, protection, and recognition. (Korostelina 2007:62,67) SIT states that the *social identity* of individuals is defined by their membership in diverse social groups which are valuable and bear emotional significance to them (Tajfel in Brown 2000:311) and where they develop and emphasize attributes inherent to the groups, as well as a positive social identity that differentiates them from other groups they do not pertain to. The higher the importance of the individual is projected, the stronger the identification with the in-group, and the more positive the difference from the out-groups. If the comparison falls negative for the individual, he/she will take action in order to change his/her own negative evaluation into a positive one. The result is obtained on the basis of four processes: *categorizations, social comparisons, distinctiveness and social identification with the in-group,* in the permanent struggle of the individuals and groups to achieve a positive position compared to others. Thus, SIT tries to respond to two main questions: how the short term identity given by group membership contributes to shaping the individuals'' core social identity, and cements it by the enumerated 4 situational processes; and to the question regarding which reasons and needs enhance the preparedness of individuals/groups to enter conflicts and competitions[14].

The key concepts of SIT enjoy a high degree of applicability in explaining the mechanisms evolving behind the securitizing move. *Categorization*[15] is defined as being a subjective cognitive process which simplifies the perception of the environment by structuring a high diversity of stimuli into a more accessible number of definite and meaningful categories, generating thus a clear focus on certain aspects which accentuate the distinction and the similarities between them, and providing a better orientation and definition of the individual''s place in society. (Hogg 1988:19, Tajfel in Worchel 1986:16) The categorization process applies to both physical and social level, and is effective particularly when it has immediate relevance to the self appraisal being one of the causes of simplified, stereotypical judgment, employed on the in-groups, the

---

[13] This categorization pertains to the Boston College, accessed on 25th.01.2009.
http://wfnetwork.bc.edu/glossary_entry.php?term=Social%20Identity%20Theory,%20Definition(s)%20of&area=All
[14] Conflicts and competitions are the infringement of social levels: entities take their issues out of their boundaries, causing them to become also issues of other entities. i.e. ranking, distribution, value conflicts (see Zick 2008:389)
[15] This notion is also put in use by Doise.

own self and on the out-groups. The consequence is a perception of the environment in terms of „we" and „they", whereas the individual perceives himself as being identical with the group and by doing this the individual „transforms" into the group itself (depersonalization). (Hogg 1988:20,21) In addition, he perceives the out-groups more homogeneous than they are in reality, having a generalized image about them.

The activated process subsequent to the identification of the self with the group is that of *social comparison*[16] as the in-group is not sole. This mechanism accentuates or even exaggerates the distinctiveness between the in-group and the out-group, trying to place the in-group into a positive position compared to the out-group, and to grant it a positive social identity. The positive distinctiveness motivates the individuals to maintain their membership into the in-group. In case the comparison falls negative for the in-group, the members of the group may try to initiate actions to turn the comparison positive. The action alternatives are translated into 3 ways:

1. *Social mobility* (switching to other group, because group boundaries are flexible);

2. *Social creativity* (since group boundaries are unbreakable, the individual finds strategies to improve the in-group"s status, a cognitive alternative to the status quo. The options are: redefining the negative evaluated characteristics; adopting new dimensions of comparison; changing the out-group);

3. *Social competition* (the direct confrontation with the out-group). (Hogg 1988:27-28, Taylor/Moghaddam 1994:84, Tajfel in Worchel 1986:9)

The *social identification with the in-group* is thus a predictor for one"s behavior towards the out-groups, since this is determined by the feeling of membership in the in-group. The mere identification with the in-group and the categorization of „we" and „them" suffice for a discriminative thinking and acting towards the out-group, and a favoring of the in-group, which "are ways to achieve for one"s own group a positive outcome of an intergroup comparison."(Mummendey 1995:660) The identification with the in-group brings about pride of belonging to the group and commitment to it, and triggers crisis when the in-group is discriminated. The stronger the social identification with one"s group the more compensatory the membership becomes, when the individual experience is negative. The social identification goes hand in hand with the *social distinctiveness*, since the former comprises the latter, individuals manifesting general tendencies to reach them both, as they are both crucial for their positive

---

[16] The concept was previously employed by Festinger in 1954, and extended by Tajfel and Turner. Festinger"s fundament for the theory was his interpreting the self-definition in notions of social identity achieved as a social comparison which reflects the outcome of the individual"s strive to achieve a satisfactory image of himself. (Tajfel 1978:68)

social identity. Thus, social identity is an intervening social mechanism in situations of social change, and the effects of these changes on their subsequent intergroup behavior and attitudes. (Tajfel 1974:76)

1.2.2 Fritz Heider's Social Balance Theory

The theory starts with the observation that the individual is situated in a causal network of the environment, which has 2 facets: the mediation that is the part close to the skin of the organism, the stimuli that act upon the organism and the influence of the person upon the environment. The second facet is the distal environment comprising vitally relevant persons and things. The mediation separates the individual from the distal environment, but also sets up a functional connection by the diverse variety of mediating events: sentiments, thoughts, wishes, emotions, and other perceptual abilities. Individuals direct their perceptions and actions to the content of the distal environment. The proximal event is interpreted in terms of relatively invariant contents of the environment, which means that individuals have definite ideas about fittingness, consonance and dissonance and the possible conditions and effects of the various existentially significant modifications and entities. The implicit knowledge of the conditions allows the distal parts of the environment to be influenced in purposeful actions. Thus Heider's theoretical scheme is an implicit model of perception, motivation, action, and norms. (Heider 1959:296-298)

For Heider, the sentiment (liking/disliking) is the connection to a diversity of situations. Two entities form a balanced unit if they are perceived as belonging together in a harmonious manner, without stress, with no pressure of change. Attitudes, beliefs, similarities, familiarity, homogeneity, proximity, interaction, common goals, property, interdependence, benefit, etc bring them together. Accordingly, the relations can be sentiment relations and unit relations[17]. They can be weakened or strengthened, yet both tend towards harmony, stability, and balance. Unbalanced situations are non-units. There are two kinds of unbalanced situations: the temporary, positive ones usually sought for escaping the boredom of the equilibrium, and to seek adventures that stimulate to further thinking; and the negative ones of distance, conflict, separateness, shortly: disunity. No matter of which kind the non unit is, as long as balance does not exist, the situation will tend to achieve balance. (Heider 1959:175-218)

---

[17] Sentiment relation refers to a unit on the base of attitudes, beliefs, and common goals. Unit relation refers to physical belonging.

Heider"s theory advances dyadic and triadic balanced and unbalanced relation models. His assumptions are that a 3 element-constellation is balanced, when 0 or 2 negative relations exist in it, and the relations need not be changed so as to function. A 3 element-constellation is unbalanced if 1 or 3 negative relations exist in it. In order the triad to become functional one negative relation necessarily needs to turn positive. I.e. John loves his girlfriend Jane, but Jane hates his friend James, whom John highly appreciates. Thus, the three can never come together without tensions. In order the system to function, either Jane changes her attitudes towards James,

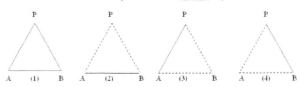

or John and James put an end to their friendship. The positive relations are symbolized by continuous lines whereas negative relations are drawn with interrupted lines. (Herkner 1991:254)

These triangles can form subcategories (semi-cycles), represented by inner lines, if another element is added, which is related to all 3 already existing elements. The same rule applies to the newly ensued triangles.

The index of balance can be conferred values from 0 – 1. The index = 0 if no semi-cycle is balanced, and = 1, if all semi-cycles are balanced. The index formula = the number of balanced semi-cycles/the number of semi-cycles.

The three folded unity can be found also in the securitization constellation is formed, which can be represented by means of cycles (the outside lines) and semi-cycles (the inner lines).

2. The Consideration of the Functional Actor from the Perspective of the 'Auxiliary Theories'

The securitization theory states that for a successful securitization, three elements should be considered: the securitizing actor, the threat to the referent object, and the functional actor, whereas the threat to the referent object is implicitly a threat to the functional actor. In order to accept the completion of securitization, the functional actor should manifest some features that are considered hereby as deducible from its in-group situation and which are reflected in it being counter-posed to the out-group, the threat source.

2.1 The Functional Actor's Position in the Securitization Constellation

As the consideration of the securitization constellation bases on the hypothesis that significant aspects of the actors" identity[18] may be deduced from their relation to each other (and from their belonging to specific groups), this chapter proposes the arrangement of each actor according to Heider"s theoretical model, by which the positions of the actors could be profiled generically in order to facilitate the analysis consistent with SIT.

Buzan asserts that "a securitizing move can easily upset orders of mutual accommodation among units[19]", and places „the survival of collective units and principles as the defining core of security studies". (Buzan 1998:27) Because of this assertion, the consideration of the actors starts from the premise that they are groups, since "to disaggregate everything into individuals is not very helpful." (Buzan 1998:40) In addition, given the categorization of securitization as extreme politics against threat sources, "the more intense [...] the dichotomization of the social world into clearly distinct and non-overlapping categories[20] , the more likely it is that the individuals who are members of the opposite group will behave toward each other in terms of groups, rather than in terms of self, as a function of their respective group membership, rather than in terms of their individual characteristics or inter-individual relationships, [...] and their actions "are likely to appear in the form of unified group actions." (Tajfel in Worchel 1984:8-11) Moreover, the conscience of common fate [21] determines individuals not to be oriented towards personal objectives, but rather towards group objectives that pursue the development of political ideologies. (Berkowitz in Tajfel 1982a:113)

Groups are subsequently generically defined as "a cognitive entity that is meaningful to the individual at a particular point in time", (Tajfel 1974:69) when they also "perceive themselves to

---

[18] Identity = hereby interpreted as „individual characteristics which become manifest or can be derived on the ground of FA"s (consciousness of its) position in what is presented in this paper as securitization scheme."
[19] Buzan defines „units" as "actors composed of various subgroups, organizations, communities, and many individuals and sufficiently cohesive and independent to be differentiated from others and to have standing at the higher levels (e.g. states, nations, transnational firms)." (Buzan 1998:6)
[20] Hornstein in Tajfel 1974:88.
[21] The proof of the sense of common fate is given in the consent to the initiation of the securitizing act.

be members of the same social category, share the [...] emotional involvement in this common definition of themselves, and achieve some degree of social consensus about the evaluation of their group. [...] Any behavior displayed by [...] actors toward [...] others is based on the actor''s identification of themselves and the others as belonging to different social categories". (Sherif in Worchel 1986:15) The definition is both categorical and dynamic since it operates in two directions: it is constructed mainly on the dynamic base, when defining the dyad „securitizer – functional actor'', and it is built on the categorical criteria in the case of the dyad „threat actor – functional actor''.[22]

The actors'' relation-diagram infers from the indications that the functional actor is neither the referent object, nor the securitizing actor, and that the referent object is not the securitizing actor. The three are in a positive unit-relation, whereas the referent object - the socially constituted unit with the claim to survival – is subject to a threat (Buzan 1998:43). According to Heider''s theory, the functional actor would be in a positive relation of dependence with the referent object (a positive unit relation, or a positive sentiment''s relation) because they cannot exist without the other. The securitization theory asserts that the referent object is in the situation of peril, without making any reference to the source of danger. The source of danger can be termed „threat source'' since threat "always points to something that is a source of danger and declares its intention of or a determination to inflict or harm others (or is presented to have such intentions, as in the case of the securitizing moves). It stresses the potential of activities of the source of danger and the ability [...] to adversely affect a specific target. [...] Out-group threat reflects negative or aggressive intentions towards the in-group. It can be real or perceived, but always affects the behavior of in-group. (Korostelina 2007:138,139)

They both (securitizer and functional actor) are in a relation of negative dependence with the threat actor because the gain of the one is the loss of the other, and they cannot achieve their goal together, which causes negative and aggressive attitudes toward the other. (Herkner 1991:490) This determines their relation to the source of the threat to be negative, and motivates them to engage as a collectivity in extreme actions and "self-reinforcing rivalries" with the source of the threat in order to protect the referent object, such interactions strengthening the „we-feeling'' of the two actors". (Buzan 1998:37) Since the source of threat is acknowledged as an actor, it can be assumed that it strives for the possession of the referent object, or its removal from the property

---

[22] The categorical definition is based on the characteristics,whereas the dynamic definition is based on the situation/interaction: The difference between the two is that in the case of the categorical definition, the individuals share the same characteristics, which, in case they are absent causes the exclusion from the group or non-inclusion in the group. Characteristics are crucial. In the case of the dynamic definition, the categorisation comes on the ground of interrelation in order to achieve a common goal. Characteristics do not matter. The dynamic definition of group cohesion differs from Turner''s model of social cohesion, where he states that individuals form groups on the bases of mutual attraction. (Wagner/Stellmacher 2000:5)

of the functional actor (or its simple damage so as to affect the latter). It results an antagonism between the securitizer and the functional actor who form a securitization block on the one hand, and the threat actor which forms the other block. The element which imbalances the constellation is the joint share of the referent object[23], respectively that all actors have a „positive" relation to the referent object, which cannot be continued in this formula. The Israel/Palestine conflict over the territory could exemplify the triangle, as both claim the right to live on the disputed land. A translation of the triangle into a Palestinian version would place in the „securitizer-functional actor" block the Hamas and the Palestinian people, whereas the threat actor would be Israel/the Israeli forces.

The social competition seems to be the adequate possibility to maintain the positive social status in relevant dimensions. Should the referent object be lost, then a relevant dimension in the self-concept of the functional actor, a distinguishing feature, disappears. (Abrams 1990:3,4) This situation is worsened as the referent object passes to another actor, which enhances its status to the detriment of the functional actor, and it would not be possible for the in-group to maintain the positive distinctiveness in the social comparison with the out-group. (Abrams 1990:3) If this threat occurs, the members whose social identity is/becomes salient would be determined to act as group members. (Abrams 1990:4)

The positioning of the actors of the securitization theory in relation to each other would result in the first triangle of the scheme. Applying the mathematical formula[24], it results that the relation is rather unbalanced → 2:4 = 0,5. The imbalance is brought by the semi-cycles (inner triads), since the cycle (outside triad) is balanced. In order to improve the balance, at least one dyad has to become different. As the threat induced by the threat actor on the referent object refers to the functional actor's identity, the relation between the two actors is highly polarized, and is unlikely to change, quite on contrary the resistance and hostility towards the source of the threat would be enhanced.[25] Also the relation of the threat actor with the securitizing actor would not change, since the securitizing actor forms a positive unit relation with the functional actor, (and at least a positive sentiment relation with the referent object) which impedes a modification of the dyad with the threat actor. Either both dyads of the outside triad change, in order to restore balance, or they keep the status quo. Under these circumstances and since the change of the dyads „functional actor – referent object" or „securitizer – referent object" would not improve the situation for the two – but rather worsen it for the functional actor, only the relation between the threat actor and the referent object can be subject to change. This dyad would have to turn negative (2nd triangle),

---

[23] or an aggregate positive relation to the referent object
[24] The index of balance = number of balanced semi-cycles/ the number of semi-cycles. 0=unbalanced; 1=balanced
[25] This is Sherif's conclusion regarding the consequences of competition for limited resources on the inter-group attitudes.

so as to admit the referent object to be shared undisturbed by the securitizer and the functional actor. Otherwise, the relation of the securitizer and of the functional actor to the referent object would be damaged (the dyads would turn negative). Thence, the calculation of the triads would reflect an improvement in the balance of the relations (4:4 = 1).

The explanation why the dyad „functional actor-securitizer" is unlikely to change is given by the securitization theory itself. It is stated that they form a unit of reciprocal determinism, where the existential threat is established inter-subjectively, and the securitizing act being negotiated, since it represents a self-violation of rules, and cannot be realized only by one of the actors. (Buzan 1998:25,26) The securitizing actor depends on the functional actor, as the acceptance of securitization is always a matter of political choice, whereas the functional actor represents its

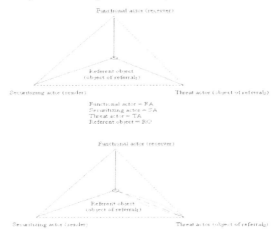

social capital, with the sole role of (dis)approving the presented measures[26]. What is more is that the functional actor depends likewise on the securitizer, as it relies on the success of the measures. In this context, they cannot elude each other for they do not dispose of the same possibilities. This implies a mutual recognition of roles and positions in face of a higher, common goal which they can achieve only together.[27]

The triangles facilitate a normative understanding of the constellation, and of the behavior of the functional actor, since the scheme implies that the functional actor (together with the securitizer) would initiate those actions necessary to insure that the referent object remains in a positive unit relation with them, and that the positive (unit) relation of the referent object to the threat actor turns negative, as this would restore balance in the constellation. The higher the referent object"s

---

[26] What these measures are depends on the nature of the threat and of the sphere it occurs. (Emmers 2007:114)
[27] The transfer of the issue from one actor to the other reflects the constructivist approach of the Copenhagen School to the security concept, as it makes securitization a political decision resulting from a political and a social act. (Emmers 2007:114)

meaning to the functional actor, the more intense the motivation to act, and the extremer the decisions/actions are likely to become.

2.2 A Possible Classification of the Functional Actor

Given being the qualification of the functional actor to allow the state"s mobilization of forces, and the employment of special powers to handle existential threats, (Buzan 1998:21) it surprises that the theory does not describe this actor nearer than being the securitizer"s „social capital". According to SIT an explanation to this phenomenon could be that "the social identity of those who dominate will be defined in terms of „subjects" and of those who are dominated in terms of „objects". The former do not think of themselves as being determined by their group membership [...]. They see themselves above all [...] singular „subjects", voluntary actors, free and autonomous, (who just form) a collection of persons. This is not the case for the dominated who are defined as undifferentiated elements in a collection of impersonal particles, and are thought of as „objects" rather than „subjects"". (Deschamps in Tajfel 1982b:90) In the securitization theory the securitizer is evidently positioned as superior and dominating. The functional actor is for the securitizer only the instrument which legitimizes its actions, with a well established auxiliary role, which actually justifies it not being detailed at all within the securitization theory.

The superiority of the securitizer might be induced by the fact that, in order to be legitimate in placing an issue high on the political agenda, it has to hold the right dominant position - of authority, but must not be an official authority[28]. (Buzan 1998:33) It has to have access to „privileged" information which gives him the opportunity to acknowledge their significance, previous to the functional actor and identify also further threats as emanating from other referent objects. (Buzan 1998:43) Buzan (1998:30) compares it in this respect to a successful diplomat, inducing the discrepancy in the positions of the two actors: "good statesmanship has to understand the threshold at which other actors feel threatened and therefore more generally to understand how the world looks to those actors". This capacity heaves and distinguishes it from the functional actor who depends on the information to understand the existential threat, turning the securitizing actor into a leader of the specific situation. Since the securitizer must not always be a statesman, being decided according to the field of securitization, and of the addressees, one such actor can be the media. I.e. the media in Israel, relating about the Palestinian situation: in

---

[28] The relation between the two usually vary „dramatically with the position held by the actor"(Buzan 1998:31). They are neither equal nor identical in all the fields of the societal life, depending on the sphere of activity, the security issues (threats), the referent object, the reasons, the conditions, etc.

2003 80% of all Israeli adults read regularly a daily newspaper, 60% watched the main television news every evening, compared to only about 40%, in the US. (Peri 2004:3 in Hass 2009:3,9)

Nevertheless the position of the functional actor is to be regarded only half-way as subordination, since it is reflects not so much its external status, but rather its being subject to an information assemblage prepared on the basis of the securitizer"s cognitive evaluation of the threat, who gains thus, an interpretative and a perspective-designing function for the audience. It presents „vulnerabilities" as „threats" and thereby as securitized, causing civil society actors to be „prisoners of their own fears",[29] in contrast to which the state is invested with increased powers and authority (Grayson 2003:339), and likewise, it does draw the outline of the future, making the functional actor aware that there is a positive alternative to the likely occurring disadvantageous situation. Yet, to convince the functional actor, it does not suffice to name the threat; it needs a persuasive rhetoric which it obtains by the reflection of the threat either in form of an indivisible conflict, or at least a divisible conflict of particular harshness, that cannot be negotiated upon, as it affects the existence basis of the functional actor. This creates the possibility for the functional actor to consent, to act as an ‚authoritative forums of decision making" and compensates partly the asymmetry between the two, seeing that it highlights the power position of the functional actor (sovereignty), which approves and legitimizes extraordinary measures to deal with the issue. (Roe 2008:616)

The asymmetrical relation of the two can be easier captured if the actors were categorized in 2 classes: institutionalized (i.e. the state, the civil society) or not institutionalized (i.e. the people, ad hoc groups), the relation between the two, being accordingly intra-institutionalized, inter-institutionalized, semi-institutionalized or non-institutionalized, displaying the particular rules of conduct.[30] The distinction could be useful in the analysis of securitization in the context in which, by the extension of the securitization theory on the non-military sector, this does not specify what kind of legitimization is necessary for the extraordinary measures, whereas the social psychological engagement is different for the two classes. In the case of the intra/inter-institutionalized relation, where the functional actor offers formal legitimization, the hierarchical positions of the two actors are clearly established, yet here, the instrumental reasons for acting may be prior to the social psychological motivation. When the functional actor is non-institutionalized, or in the cases the relation is semi-institutionalized, the relation of superiority and inferiority become relative, but the social psychological aspects may predominate. Who the securitizer (the one authorized to initiate extraordinary measures or to raise the awareness of the

---

[29] i.e. "individuals, politicians, decision-makers, and media actors, who misuse the feelings of fear and exaggerate threats to pursue selfish aims, or to legitimate violations against international law and human rights", employing a one side perception stategy in rendering facts. (Hass 2009:3,14)
[30] This also corresponds to the apprehension of the functional actor on social-political and social-psychological level of analysis.

threat) or the functional actor is, decides each particular situation for itself, since each field has its particular institutions, organizations and participating individuals. Nonetheless, if the institutions differ than the non-institutional actors are very similar independently of the branch, for their membership and meaning of the „securitized environment" are determined by the internal motivations of the individuals.

The non-institutionalized functional actor (i.e. the public) may provide informal legitimization, but does not have the competence to offer „formal" support that „mandates governments to adopt a specific policy". (Balzacq in Roe 2008:616) The people are important, but sometimes not the most important, since their role differs according to the political system and the nature of the issue. Formal legitimization can be given only by institutions. Still, both categories are vital in the

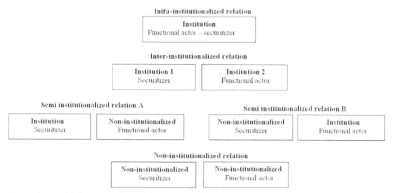

launching of securitizing acts, the achievement of both on the part of the securitizer increasing the chances of successful securitization. (Roe 2008:620) According to Balzacq "securitizing agents always strive to convince as broad an audience as possible because they need to maintain a social relationship with the target individual group. [...] Political officials are responsive to the fact that winning formal support while breaking social bonds with constituencies can wreck their credibility. That explains why, while seeking formal acquiescence, political officials also cloak security arguments in the semantic repertoire of the national audience in order to win support." (Balzacq quoted in Roe 2008:620)

The institutionalized functional actors are much more marginalized in the securitization process, than non-institutionalized functional actors, since the securitizer bares a certain degree of legitimacy, on the base of the existing procedures. In this case, the formal, hierarchical aspects do play a higher role than the social psychological criteria, and could reflect how securitization is a self-referential practice. According to Roe (2008:618), „the military sector of security often carries with it a certain degree of legitimacy in terms of the government"'s – or, more precisely, the military"'s – ability to act without the consent of the general public and/or other securitizing audiences. This is particularly so in the case of pre-emptive or covert military strikes – for example, where the need exists for operational details to be kept secret because of the danger of revealing vital information to the enemy."

The institutionalization of a threat occurs, according to the Copenhagen School if the threat is recurrent. (Buzan 1998:27) In this case, once the formal legitimization is given, the continuation of other securitizing acts is facilitated, on the ground of the first consent of the functional actor. This makes subsequent reiteration of „securitizing moves" secondary, and bearing an intensified informing character, meant to keep the alert system of the securitizing institution at least „high, if not severe"[31]. In this kind of relation the wide public is mainly excluded, or not taken into consideration as decisive factor, the policy being unwound at „high/restricted level", even if the issue concerns directly the people.

In the case of the non-institutionalized functional actor, the prolongation of securitization must be reiterated by the securitizer, in order to motivate again its necessity on the base of the functional actor's position related to the threat source and to persuade it. This maintains the state of tension and crisis by instilling or maintaining the fear in the functional actor, inasmuch as the continuation of securitization is a consequence of fear of possible negative events. Addressing a non-institutionalized functional actor reflects better the inter-subjectivity of securitization and its combination with self-referentiality, as it bases to a greater extent on the social psychological processes that individuals undergo in society in order to establish their position, value and power. In like manner addressing a non-institutionalized functional actor reflects better the social psychological fusion of 2 actors (systems) in a joint venture against the source of threat.

The semi institutionalized relation between the securitizer and the functional actor brings together the two levels of actors and expresses best how securitization is a process that implies both state institutions and citizens, and that the most efficient securitization is that which combines both the formal and the informal legitimization, covering the entire range of necessary and consistent feedback for the initiation of actions beyond normal politics. Thus, this type of relation is the most complex one and offers the securitizing move the highest chances for success.

If the processes within an institution can be observed from outside only with a certain degree of difficulty (i.e. the army), since the outsiders witness usually only their outcome, than the processes in semi-institutionalized or non-institutionalized relations offer a higher insight

---

[31] Here: high degree of alert = high probability that the threat actor would intervene against the referent object; severe alert = imminent danger from the threat actor. (Alert system adapted from the Security Advisory System of the U.S. Department of Homeland Security http://www.terror-alert.com/)

potential. If for institutional functional actors formalities and regulations are decisive in establishing the conduct, than for non-institutional actors social aspects gain priority.

2.3   Features Resulting From the In-Group Processes

The functional actor''s consent to the securitization act is an indices that the functional actor has crossed the key processes of definition and assessment of its social identity, since only their outcome can support the functional actor's justification for conflict, (Zick 2008:413) and its engagement in whatever actions necessary to protect the referent object and thus the integrity of the in-group. This implies first of all that the functional actor has dimensioned its reality in dichotomous terms, that is, in an in-group – out-group paradigm, and organizes its behavior accordingly, being in favor of the in-group, as affected group, accentuating its (psychological and behavioral) involvement with the in-group (the securitizer and the referent object), and asserting the adversity towards the out-group, as the threat source. (Worchel 1986:12)

The consent to the securitizing act implies not a whatsoever identification with the in-group, but a high degree of identification (strong psychological engagement), since this is a prerequisite for engagement in extreme actions for the group''s sake. According to the field studies of Simon et al. (1998) the level of identification of the individuals with the affected in-group is a reliable predictor of collective action[32]. (Simon in Brown 2000:332) "The more they identify (with the group), the less they want to leave (it)". (Ellemer in Brown 2000:327) This would also serve as an indicator for the functional actor's engagement readiness in the causes of the group and may reflect its perception of the in-group: a high status group, since these tend more to display a cooperative behavior than low status groups. (Hogg/Terry 2001:154, Tyler 2000:149)

SIT states that high-status groups tend to show more in-group bias than low-status groups (Brown 2000:323), whereas low-status groups tend to dissatisfaction with the in-group, out-group favoritism, and even „disidentification" with the in-group.[33] (Brown 2000:325,327, Ellemers 2002:249). There are also low status groups that manifest similar attitudes towards its group, as the members of high status groups. Still, this occurs only when the in-group is a powerful source of self-esteem and pride, or when the group is the prime identity supplier[34]. Usually, the most

---

[32] Another predictor is the endorsement of the political goals, in the situations when the in-group situation is perceived as unjust and potentially open to change.
[33] The distinction between high and low status groups should be regarded as being a subjective one, since it does not reflect so much the objective reality, but the perception of the members of the group.
[34] A primary identity is that for which an individual would sacrifice most of his time/money, and even his life. A secondary identity is for which the individual would sacrifice only some of his time/money. For a tertiary identity, the individual would be willing to sacrifice only some of his time and perhaps a little money. (Singer - Intercultural Communication: A Perceptual Approach)

probable attitude of low-status groups is: „if you can't beat them, join them" (Tajfel in Brown 2000:326), being difficult to mobilize, since they see the heterogeneity within the in-group, perceive themselves more as separate individuals and by this, they see the impediments for effective collective actions.[35] (Tajfel in Ellemers 2002:253) Members of high status groups are more willing to engage in favor of the group, since the high status is the source of a more favorable social identity and of higher feelings of self-esteem and self-worth. This enhances their cooperation willingness in case of the securitizing act. (Tyler 2000:151)

This is not the case in the securitization theory, as the functional actor approving of proceeding against the threat source[36] manifests a sense of responsibility for the protection of its in-group (Buzan 1998:29) standing as a high identifier, since it is more likely to assist its group and is more willing to expend individual effort intended to improve the group"s position, as the membership to the group is a source of pride and self-esteem, and its self-concept and/or its social identity is depending on the in-group"s status. (Zick 2008:414,421) This reflects that the in-group is highly representative for the individual and interchangeable with it, (Turner in Worchel 1998:128) that the values and goals of the group have been internalized, with the consequence of the enhancement of thinking in terms of group interests rather than in terms of individual interests, the support being offered, even if it might contradict individual concerns, these being placed prior to the personal values and interests. (Tajfel 1982b:26,29) Accordingly there takes place a display of behavioral depersonalization,[37] respectively an attitudinal and behavioral uniformity with the rest of the group-members, the behavior increasing its normative level directly proportional with the degree of the group"s salience. (Abrams 1990:15)

The higher the identification with the group, the higher the commitment to the value of the referent object and thus to the success in protecting it, on behalf of the functional actor is to be expected. The commitment represents a positive attachment to the group and/or referent object, because of the sense that it is a source of a positive identity and internally motivates the voluntary engagement to whatever actions necessary to support the in-group. (Tyler 2000:164) This attitude leads to the internal desire to get involved in the group"s affairs, reflecting the inner forces that drive the actions. (Tyler 2000:55-56) Should commitment lack, than the case becomes that of an individualistic mentality, which is characterized by that it does not engage for the enhancement of

---

[35] Still, there has to be taken into consideration, that in individualistic cultures, the in-group identity is not so developed as in collectivistic cultures. (Tajfel 1974:86,97)
[36] The afore mentioned attitude of low-status groups does not count when the low-status in-group regards the intergroup boundaries unbreakable, as in the case of ethnicity, gender, color, which as a consequence affects the identification with the in-group. (Conclusions of Ellemer et al. 1997 reproduced by Brown 2000:327)
[37] This accentuates the group prototypicality, stereotypicality or normativeness of people, and is a process underlying the group cohesion, ethnocentrism, cooperation, altruism, emotional contagion, empathy, collective behavior, shared norms and mutual influence process. (Abrams 1990:12)

the collective wellness, but for its own interest, whereas securitization represents rather an activity for the interest of a collectivity.

Commitment is closely related to the feelings of loyalty, the functional actor may be presumed to manifest towards the referent object, since the engagement in the securitization act is a reflection of the hold with the securitizer. Like in the case of commitment, the degree of loyalty is a good predictor for the engagement of the functional actor in extraordinary measures, for it is usually a consequence of the dependence on the referent object (or the securitizer). (Tyler 2000:56, Hogg/Terry 2001:254) This loyalty can be dedicated to the securitizer, the functional actor''s group, to the referent object or to the values this represents, and which the functional actor shares itself. To this there could be added the satisfaction with the referent object and its value for the functional actor, which is also a prerequisite in dedication to the group''s problem-solving. This goes back on the intrinsic interest of the functional actor with the group''s position and role based on the referent object up to the moment of the securitizing move, and reflects the association of the self and its concerns with the group and its concerns, the referent object and its meaning being a source of self-satisfaction. (Tyler 2000:56,57)

The above mentioned sense of responsibility, commitment, loyalty towards the in-group, interchangeability of the individual with the group are yet present only when a strong social salience is given. These are conditions that facilitate the readiness to defense of the ideals and values of the in-group by means that do not exclude violence and conflict. Given being the significance of the consent to the securitizing act, it could be deduced that the referent object and its meaning for the functional actor are salient for it, since on contrary, the fate of the referent object would remain to some extent neglected. According to 2 studies effectuated by Korostelina on two groups of Russians and Crimean Tatars (2007:57), salience influences attitudes and perceptions in the sense that it enhances prejudicial thinking and produces a powerful internal motivation for action, being the most important determinant of identity. Salience precedes and determines the readiness for conflict behavior, i.e. in the case of ethnicity or the norms and values of religious groups. (Korostelina 2001:74,78)

Group salience bears a great impact on social identity especially in collectivistic cultures, where the strong belonging to a group is defining. The focus on the group reflects a pride based categorical social self. The opposite would be the respect based reputational social self that is directed towards the individual and its unique features. The difference between the two is that while the pride based group develops strong connections between the individual and the group, its members being expected to engage in difficult and dangerous situations to protect the group, the respect based group encourages individual, personalized conducts. Judging on these coordinates, the (group of the) functional actor is part of the pride based category, since the engagement in extraordinary measures may be the result of loyalty and affection to the referent object, the referent object denoting in such case a high mobilization capacity in periods of crisis, when it manifests a sense of obligation or duty to support the group. The other category is rather weak in situations of crises, because it has difficulties in maintaining common group goals, but being prolific in cases of creativity, when everyone is following its own ideas. Since securitization is not a case of creativity but rather of direct challenge and crisis, the downsides of the pride based group may be well visible in the demeanor of the functional actor: out of the attitudes towards the referent object it may engage in illegal actions on behalf of it, focusing on its necessities and internal norms rather than on external norms, such as law, or even personal moral principles. (Hogg/Terry 2001:160-163) Under these circumstances, the more powerful the sense of obligation or duty, the more it could defer to rules that restrict their freedom of behavior. (Tyler 2000:66)

The pride based categorical self of the functional actor may explain its proactive, engaging discretionary behavior for the benefit of the group, since securitization is an act of voluntary decision, an expression of an externally consistent value system of those who engage in it, based on attitudes and values oriented towards collectivism which function as an internal motivational source for the involvement in collective actions. (Personal and communal values do not contradict each other). (Hogg/Terry 2001:151). The roots of discretionary behavior lie in the attitudes and values of the functional actor. They shape the voluntary and self-regulatory behavior (Hogg/Terry 2001:161) that support a positive sense of themselves, and provide a framework of their judgments, determining responses of the judging in cases of simple comparisons and evaluations, but also in cases of threat to these values when they intervene to protect them. I.e. the membership in the Lebanese guerilla Hezbollah which forced the Israeli withdrawal from the country, has become a source of inspiration for thousands Lebanese Shia who turned members, and won the respect of other religious communities, being a powerful source of pride.

The consequence of the above mentioned attitudes is the sense of prototypicality, a specificity of high identifiers with the in-group. According to SIT this has double effect. On the one hand it influences attribution and information processing, triggering stereotypical thinking; on the other hand, it raises the influential basis for the perception of those apprehended as being prototypical. (Hogg/Terry 2001:202-204) This becomes most evident when group members face group threat or competition. In these circumstances, individuals would incline to concentrate on shared features (self-stereotyping categorization), making intra-group distinctions irrelevant, (Abrams 1990:14) and even exaggerating the perception of mutual similarity. i.e. the Bosnian population regard the nationalist parties as the sole „typical" Bosnian alternative to the international actors, which did not meet the Bosnian interests properly, and identify their interests as their own, supporting their policies. (Gentile 2008:18) According to Fishman, "an ideologized position can minimize seemingly major differences or ignore them entirely [...] because they relate to a superordinate value" (Fishman in Tajfel 1974:75), which facilitates several in-group processes that serve subsequently for the justification of extreme actions radical judgments and group-polarization[38]. These are, among others cohesion, emotional empathy or contagion, persuasion, cooperation, mobilization, etc. (Abrams/Hogg 1990:13) When this similarity is given, "the amount of the in-group bias increases" which creates an antagonism between their interests and thus between the groups (Brown 2000:326) and may predict the group members" (positive) behavioral responses to the securitizing move, since the extreme actions are collective actions. (Ellemers 2002:252).

This happens even if the relationship of the functional actor with the securitizing actor is institutionalized. If this occurs, the in-group attitudes of the functional actor would be characterized by intensification, as according to Tajfel "in-group affiliation and out-group hostility are both intensified through prolonged intra-group interaction between the subjects". (Tajfel 1974:74) These imply positive attitudes towards the securitizing actor, like trustworthiness, which also rises the degree of suggestibility or, „the attraction", as the authors of the theories of the social identity state.[39] Should contrary attitudes exist, the functional actor would turn against the securitizing actor, undergoing a backfire process, according to the boomerang effect[40]. Pursuant to its logics, a positive perceived securitizer would have more chances of success than a negative perceived one, because the functional actor would more easily change his attitude in the direction intended by the securitizer, if it respects and admires the securitizer, rather than if the perception of the is neutral or negative, in which case the securitizing move would fail. (Herkner 1991:230)

In the case that the functional actor likes the securitizer, previous interpersonal attraction is not necessary, for how much individual group members are liked depends on their perceived prototypicality, more prototypical group members being socially more attractive. Intra-group/social attraction (liking) is based in inter-group relations on perceived similarity, being more depersonalized than individual attraction. Still, liking on the base of prototypicality, functions only in groups with high salience, (Abrams 1990:21) and in case it occurs, it would

---

[38] "Polarization has been characterized as a group decision making bias, in which groups make judgements which are more extreme than the average initial position of the group members." (Abrams/Hogg 1990:15)
[39] The same conclusions where drawn also by Hovland & o. in 1953 and Walster & o. in 1966. They affirm that the trustworthiness of the source has a persuasive impact of a communication. If there is distrust the communication has a smaller impact on the acceptance of the discourse, respectively on the cooperation preparedness on the side of the listener. (Schopler 1998:86)
[40] The boomerang effect is the theory of psychological reactance, according to which people act to protect their sense of freedom (Brehm, S., & Brehm, J.W. 1981).

again point out a high degree of involvement of the functional actor with the in-group, since liking determined by prototypicality is a characteristic of high status groups. I.e. in the first phase of the external interventionism after the Dayton Agreement the positive attitude of the Bosnian population versus the nationalist forces increased, when seeing that the international interference undermined the economical and the political development of the country. (Gentile 2008:6,10) this happened as the nationalist forces were perceived as supporting the interests of the people, becoming „prototypical" for them.

The functional actor''s strong identification and involvement with the in-group is reflected also by it not considering other „cognitive alternative" to insure the referent object, and to achieve balance or consonance, than the measures beyond normal politics, which represent a direct challenge of the source of threat. I.e. the Hamas actions against the Israeli forces. This aspect has the capacity to disclose also other issues about the functional actor''s position in the constellation: according to Tajfel, this could mean either that the sense of the group-membership is so strong that social mobility would mean an internal conflict of values for the individual; or that the individual fears powerful social sanctions, by reason of which its mobility may be undesirable; or that the group''s boundaries are impermeable, and the status of the group is stable. (Tajfel 1974:82, Zick 2008:413) Such actors, display an increased degree of group-salience (Korostelina 2007:79) and opt for the direct challenge "share the basic feature of the social change system of beliefs, in the sense that the multi-group structure is perceived as characterized by the extreme difficulty or impossibility of an individual''s moving from one group to another", (Tajfel in Worchel 1986:10) considering social competition in a better light than other alternatives to solve the identity issue, an option which is actually regarded by Tajfel and Turner rather negative and destructive. This process occurs even in the case of already decaying identity and integrity of high status groups, which can be counteracted by artificially starting up a conflict with an out-group, this being vital for the maintenance of the positive identity of the in-group, since is assures the coherence and the internal stability of the group by the concentration of forces in other directions. (Zick 2008:414).

Given being the content of the securitizing move, the functional actor nonetheless, indicates by its consent to extraordinary measures, that it does not identify other more reliable way to protect its possession, not so much out of fear of social sanction from within the group, but rather out of fear of negative consequences for the in-group general position, in case of not acting. This would induce at its turn a conflict of values for the functional actor, subsequent to the loss of the referent object, since its social position would have changed unfavorably. As a consequence, the attitudes towards the referent object amplify, and would undo the social mobility option, an idea supported by argument that the functional actor has the freedom to decide whether the issue is to be subsequently politicized or securitized.

The absence of other conflict-approaches denotes not only a lack of negotiation readiness, but also a deficiency of toleration of the conflict"s status quo on behalf of the functional actor.[41] Likewise, it does indicate the functional actor"s belief in the changeableness of its condition. "The problems of the social identity [...] would not necessarily find expression in social behavior until and unless there is some awareness, that the existing social reality is not the only possible one and that alternatives to it are conceivable and perhaps attainable. If this awareness exists, the problems of social identity confronting the members [...] can be solved [...]." (Tajfel 1974:82) In these circumstances, the prospective of being deprived of the referent object has a mobilizing effect in the emergence of attitudes, intentions and actions in the conflict direction. (Tajfel 1982a:106) This presumption could indicate that the functional actor manifests a heightened form of self-consciousness and a sense of fear which goes down to the individual, even if the threat (to the referent object) manifests at group level, (Stephan 2002:197,198) which would also predict a rather destructive, deepening conflict development. The following behavior would result than in actions by which the referent object, and thereby the positive status of the functional actor would be protected, since securitization may be regarded as a cooperative behavior in the pursuit of positive identity projecting values.

The consent to the securitizing act reflects moreover that the functional actor apprehends itself as being the legitimate owner of the referent object to which it is unquestionably entitled. Accordingly, the consent is the expression of its claim for its right for the maintenance of the referent object, being uneasy at the possibility of loosing it. Durkheim considers that what it takes to maintain social order is that people are content with their fate. Yet, what it takes to make them content is [...] that they are convinced that they do not have the right for more. (Durkheim in Tajfel 1982a:115). The functional actor definitely proves the contrry. This is a motive to act, but also an enhancement of intergroup competition and stronger in-group identification.[42] (Tajfel 1982a:112-113) This goes together with the perception of the members of high status groups, that their group-status is legitimate, as an earned position of just procedure. If acknowledging a threat to this status, these are likely to engage in more negative reactions than those who view their group-status illegitimate. The fact that the individuals or their groups engage in securitization points out again that the groups are high status groups, since the low status groups, perceiving their status as legitimate are more likely to accept the situation. Only those who perceive the situation as illegitimate behave like high status groups. (Hogg:2001:242, Tyler 2000:150)

---

[41] This is supported also by the securitising move claiming a monolithic identity and thereby suppressing its flexibility and negotiability. (Gromes 2007:8)
[42] The same conclusions were drawn before by Berkowitz in experiments with Afro-Americans standing for their rights in front of white people. There were only those who saw a chance of success that fought

The functional actor perceives the threat and the new negative situation as illegitimate and unfair, which mobilizes it into collective actions, since the perceived illegitimacy is the social and psychologically accepted leverage to set into motion actions and social changes in the inter-group relations and behaviors. According to Ellemers, "group members are more inclined to engage in collective protest as they consider their group"s plight more unjust." (Ellemers 2002:245) To take as an example a frozen conflict where open violence is rather absent, the aversion being noticeable in the ideologized positions of the groups, there could be mentioned the Cypriot conflict. The Greek-Cypriot leadership considering the North of the Island as being occupied illegally by Turkey, and what Greek-Cypriot society has experienced has been a grave injustice, and an unacceptable affront to its human rights, they have sought retribution from Turkey and still regard as solution the withdrawal of Turkish troops. Accordingly, they want Turkey to be brought to justice, many individual cases being presented in front of the European Court for Human Rights. (Demetriou 2008:7,8,11). In the case of a hot conflict, like the Palestinian/Israeli one, both parts proceed with organized violent attacks against each other, since they both consider their situation unfair, and the claims of the other (threat) illegitimate. The legitimate threat would not pull the ‚group together" into collective actions, but would drive it apart and would contribute to a further politicization of the matter. (Tajfel 1982a:116,117) This belief in its right prevents the occurrence of dissonance in consenting to the extraordinary measures, and heightens its sense of responsibility. When the right to keep the referent object exists, there would be dissonance in not initiating the securitizing act, because this would bare irreversible consequences. (Festinger in Tajfel) Acting would imply that the referent object is worthy and that there is less to loose by acting than by not acting.

The perception of illegitimacy could be also a result of a policy of encouragement of the difference between the social categories, the functional actor being exposed to it as a target, and having developed a self/group-centered vision of the dichotomous society, as a consequence of the valorization of the in-group identity and position. This involves also established ideas of what its due is, and a naturally arising claim for its rights, as well as a depreciative evaluation of out-groups. i.e. the policy led by the nationalist political groups in Bosnia, but also in other conflicts. Under these conditions, the possibility of conflict escalation is inasmuch high, if the in-group feels that its dominance or rights are affected, or that the influence or the claims of the out-group are perceived as being unfunded. (Zick 2008:418,424) I.e. in the case of the Israeli belief of the right on the Palestinian Territories who fear that the return of the Palestinians would affect their living space, and thus the Jewish identity.

The consequence of this may be the sense of losing the superordinate values that the referent object represented, which bares the seeds of the readiness of the functional actor"s ignoring the internal group-conflicts and explain disposition and readiness for conflict and aggression, since by the consent to securitization, it declares itself prepared to defend the referent object with whatever actions considered necessary by the securitizer. These may involve a high mobilization of forces[43], and the risk of abuses, violation of rights, loss of control, etc, which is an indication of the functional actor"s trust in the securitizer, since securitization represents the failure of the state to have developed institutions and mechanisms to deal with existential risks in a reliable, (socially) regulated manner (Buzan 1998:29), which is contextual synonymous with the incapacity of the state"s institutions to reach a consensus regarding priorities, common interests, or even values. This failure could act as an amplifying factor for conflict readiness if it puts at risk the sense of integrity, identity, self-perception/evaluation, etc of the functional actor. In the Cypriot case this has been materialized by the appeal to the European Court for Human Right, where citizens of both parts of the island accused the Republic for the violation of their individual human rights, an issue caused by the domestic political incapacity to solve the cases. (Demetriou 2008:24)

In this respect, the consent to the securitizing act implies that the securitizing move has been a successful combination of perception, language, and intrinsic features of society and the functional actor. [44] (Buzan 1998:32) It is a confirmation that the securitizing move connected the inner reality of the securitizer (i.e. its interests) with the external one, of the functional actor, bringing the two together and having behavioral effects on the functional actor that has undergone a "social influence process in which it has been persuaded by significant others to define itself". (Tajfel 1982b:27) When an actor securitizes an issue – correctly or not – "it is a political fact that has consequences, because this securitization will cause the actor to operate in a different mode than he or she would do otherwise" (Buzan 1998:30) It influences the further actions of the functional actors, producing conformity in the group norm (convergence on the prototypical position), which are likely to be extremized depending on the social comparative context. (Abrams 1990:16)

This denotes both, the functional actor"s susceptibility to persuasion, and its over-perception of self-as-target with destructive consequences" on psychological and behavioral level: hypersensitivity, fearfulness, mistrust, dissatisfaction, hostility, etc, as it is the victim of the neglect, inability, disagreement of those responsible, etc. (Kramer in Schopler 1998:241) The susceptibility to persuasion is given by the securitization theory information that the functional actor has the liberty of decision and action and cannot be obliged to initiate extraordinary measures, in the context where there are several securitizing actors competing for the

---

[43] States of emergency always supposes mobilization of forces – especially of military ones and of the civilian authorities, high degree of caution.
[44] The explanation is best provided by Bottenberg"s codification theory.

representation of the same referent object. (Buzan 1998:45) "It is always a political choice to securitize or to accept securitization" (Buzan 1998:29) This would mean on the one hand that the accepted securitizing move conceived as a specific form of political act[45] is audience centered, in line with the functional actor"s reasoning, on account of the commonly perceived indispensability of the referent object, and of the principle that the situation of the referent object"s situation influences the judgment of the functional actor.[46] (Tyler 2000:148) In the end, "what may seem legitimate securitization within a given political community, may appear paranoid to those outside it" (Buzan 1998:30). On the second hand, that the functional actor"s group may be selected as a separate category of audience (Buzan 1998:41), depending on the issue to be decided upon, since a shared understanding is not present in the entire audience, and "what constitutes the threat for one is not necessarily the referent object for the other", (Buzan 1998:45) whereas the proposed policy responses need to achieve the required level of agreement, while audiences may also decide to reject its implications. (Roe 2008:622). Thus the functional actor is that which shares the understanding of what represents the value of the referent object, what is a security issue, (Emmers 2007:113) and on the base of common interests, forms a unit with the securitizing actor. In the case of ethnical conflicts, the functional actor may be the entity with authoritative power, manifesting radical or nationalist bias.

Only those who manifest a reciprocal contingency[47] having the same apprehension as the securitizing actor feel addressed and affected by the changing regarding the referent object. This implies the functional actor"s dynamic receptivity and responsiveness to the proposed policies in face of the changing context, a heightened self-consciousness, internalization of the in-group values and a spirit of cautiousness regarding the status of the group. (Levine p.5) Individuals manifesting this kind of features would tend to accept the radicalism of the securitizing move. For this reason, "it does matter how others judge the reasonableness of a securitization, because this influences how other actors in the system will respond to the security claim." (Buzan 1998:30) Thence the securitizer usually presents the referent object in terms of the functional actor"s identity and commonness with the securitizer, this being a strategy principle in line with Tajfel according to which individuals are influenced by „similar people who provide information about physical or social reality, about one"s social category".

Should the securitization situation not bring forth political structures to deal with the security issue according to the novel situation, than the functional actor is susceptible to manifest uncertainty and construct a new identity to deal with the changing environment massively, since

---

[45] According to Waever & Buzan a security issue is always a political construction, not an objective existing fact.
[46] The securitizing actor expects that the threat he verbalises is answered by the functional actors with the consent to the mobilization of maximum effort, which consists in extraordinary measures. (Wæver 1997:54)
[47] Other types of contingencies are: pseudo-contingency, asymmetrical contingency, reactive contingency.

social identity is the cognitive mechanism that makes group behavior possible. (Reicher in Tajfel 1982b:67) This would bring the functional actor near to the crowd behavior, which acts on the ground of common social identity, but could also lead to the formation of militant or terrorist groups, like the Hezbollah, built to end the Israeli occupation in Lebanon. That means that "there is an immediate identification with a superordinate category which defines a field of possible identities; crowd members [...] construct a specific identity which corresponds to the concrete situation". (Reicher in Tajfel 1982b:69,71) The crowd would be than characterized by a contagion of diffused ideas and emotion, in which individuals learn the specific stereotypic norms and ways of behavior, which becomes more normative (conformist) as their category membership becomes salient. (Reicher in Tajfel 1982b:72) Yet, according to the same author, the effects of contagion, will be limited to those who identified with the crowd, and the behavior will not be random, but "it will represent the adaptation to a novel situation of an historical tradition." (Reicher in Tajfel 1982b:73) Nonetheless, the crowd's behavior is „pure expression of autistically expressed fixed tendencies" (Reicher in Tajfel 1982b:74), being preoccupied intensively with the proposed goal, where the actions are formed accordingly, and the members „display feelings of almost infinite power". Under the impact of such circumstances individuals become unusually susceptible to the acceptance of new formulations that justify their behavior. (Le Bon in Tajfel 1982b:76)

The assessments of the features of the functional actor in the process of securitization could be summarized in the following figure:

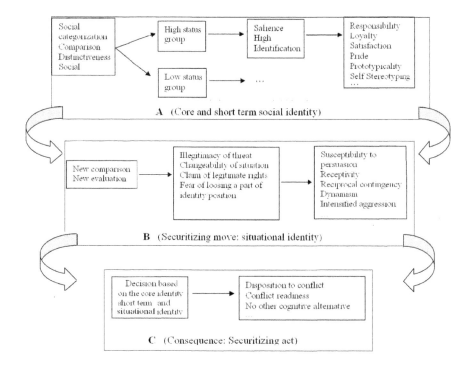

| Social categorization Comparison Distinctiveness Social | High status group / Low status group | Salience High Identification / ... | Responsibility Loyalty Satisfaction Pride Prototypicality Self Stereotyping ... |

A (Core and short term social identity)

| New comparison New evaluation | Illegitimacy of threat Changeability of situation Claim of legitimate rights Fear of loosing a part of identity position | Susceptibility to persuasion Receptivity Reciprocal contingency Dynamism Intensified aggression |

B (Securitizing move: situational identity)

| Decision based on the core identity short term and situational identity | Disposition to conflict Conflict readiness No other cognitive alternative |

C (Consequence: Securitizing act)

2.4 Features Resulting from Intergroup Processes

According to SIT, "the meaning of identity develops on the border between groups and constitutes both the content of group membership and the specificity of interrelations with out-groups." (Korostelina 2007:74) Still, the sole information about the threat actor can be deduced from the securitizing move, in which all responsibility for the threatening situation is simplistically shifted to something/somebody else, which has to be „taken care of", this category being untheorized by the designers of the securitization concept like that of the functional actor. (Grayson 2003:339) The threat actor is in an antagonistic position to the functional actor and to the securitizer, as it aims at the functional actor's referent object, which they cannot have at the same time. This places them in a relation of negative dependence and to such a degree antithetic, that the functional actor accepts the polarity synthesized by the securitizer[48], and reflecting a series of negative attitudes, of which, besides those mentioned above (low degree of tolerance,

---

[48] The assumption is backed by Freud"s view of intergroup relations, which states that "out-group hostility is a necessary condition for harmony within the in-group, since if hostile feelings are not displaced onto an outgroup, they could turn inward and destroy the in-group" (Freud presented by Taylor/Moghaddam 1994:26)

unwillingness to enter a compromise, adversity, discrimination, perception of illegitimacy and unfairness) come to be expressed first.

The attitude of the functional actor may point to the power and status relation between the two actors. According to the theses of SIT, it can be assumed that the relation between the functional actor and the threat actor is asymmetrical, as only an asymmetry can cause identity problems. This can be of power, of rank, of prestige, etc, since these differences emphasize the intergroup conflict of interests, and exacerbate the opposition of the groups. (Thibaut in Worchel 1986:11) Nevertheless, the two antagonistic groups must bare a similarity because groups enter into social comparisons and competition with similar groups. (Tajfel 1982a:106). These similarities can be given by goals, proximity (common space) and other shared issues that pose an identity threat to the in-group, because they are used as essential comparison/categorization dimensions. Under these conditions this similarity enhances not attraction, but repulsion. (Abrams/Hogg 1990:188)

The securitization theory does not say whether the position of the functional actor is in a superior or in an inferior one, it just says that it will be an inferior one, if the referent object is not secured. SIT asserts that threat is felt as coming only from a superior or at least an equal entity, whereas in the first case the difference between the two actors would not be severe, so as to permit the functional actor to react and to believe that its reaction would have the potential either protect its referent object or determine the threat actor to give up its claim on it. Should the asymmetry be extreme there would not be securitization – the functional actor being very weak, it would not engage into competition for it may lose; the functional actor being very strong, it would likewise not engage into competition, for its position makes competition pointless. In case of equality, the threat actor must have the power to threaten with inferiority that is with deprivation. This is the reason why the functional actor opts for the social competition.

Despite of the vagueness of the securitization theory on the threat actor, it can be assumed that it is in at least one way important to the functional actor since in-groups do not compare themselves with whichever group but only with those it perceives as relevant in respect to proximity and situational salience. Here, the competition is enhanced by incompatible group goals (Worchel 1986:17) i.e. the Israeli/Palestinian, the Cypriot conflict, etc. Given being the consent to the securitizing act, it may be deduced that the importance of the threat actor resides in the perception of its possibilities to damage or remove the referent object from the functional actor.

The existent competition between the two actors for the referent object influences the perception and the attitudes of the functional actor towards the threat actor. First it causes it to exaggerate the sense of competitivity, as according to Taylor and Moghaddam (1994:40), even if competitivity exists in reality to very low degree, it is likely that group opponents perceive it as higher, or expects it to be higher and thus, increase their own competitivity. Moreover, just the idea of in-group-out-group scheme, causes the participants to expect from the other rather competitiveness than (unexpected) cooperativeness". This phenomenon triggers „divisiveness", an ideological position that does not only magnify minor differences [...] but can also manufacture differences (Fishman in Tajfel 1974:75), exaggerating the cleavage to the out-group, an occurrence registered especially in case of groups, which, according to Schopler (1998:76), are generally more prone to distrust and to be distrusted than individuals. Divisiveness becomes than the antonym of proportionality in actions. This case applies even if discussions take place between the opponent group and individuals – since they represent their group positions and act on behalf of their group"s interest, and not in the personal concern, and could explain, why the functional actor/securitizing actor do not see other cognitive alternative to insure the referent object than the competition.

According to SIT, the mere encounter of two different groups or categories, determines the behavior of the individuals according to their membership to the specific groups. (Tajfel in Worchel 1998:126) Yet, the confrontation does not mean in the first instance intensive negative attitudes towards the other, in this case, the threat actor. There has to be a prerequisite for the in-group member (functional actor) to manifest extreme attitudes towards the out-group member (threat actor): "in order for the members of an in-group to be able to hate or dislike an out-group, or to discriminate against it, the former must first have acquired a sense of belonging to a group which is clearly distinct from the one (latter) they hate, dislike or discriminate against." (Tajfel 1974:66) This prerequisite is given conscientiously at least through the securitizing move, which, recalling negative facts to the disadvantage of the functional actor enhances negative dispositions that create a fertile ground for other negative attitudes, judgments, and actions towards the source of threat. These are inasmuch intensified since the securitizing move induces that the functional actor does not have the choice in confronting the threat, for this was decided upon by the threat actor, presumed to have bad intentions.[49] I.e. The Israeli security wall is presented by the Israeli government as having a non-permanent character and a mere security purpose. Due to the Israeli policy in the last 50 years, the Palestinians are convinced that its real purpose is to mark a future border, and in addition to that it is considered to cut the human rights of many Palestinians by preventing them from going to their agricultural land or to the next hospital, (Hass 2009:8)

The fact that the other is a strategic actor with several choices and goals (of which it chose the negative ones) "is an amplifying factor in any threat-perception and therefore assists in pushing an issue across the security threshold [...] because the other is an actor [...] it has the potential of

---

[49] Bandura talks of unjustified (subjective) damage vs. justified (objective) damage. Only the unjustified damage can trigger the aggression of the victim, since it goes back on the bad intentions of the aggressor. Objective damage does not have a powerful aggression triggering potential, since it is attributed to causes independent of the aggressor.

outwitting us, of having intentions, or of bending or suppressing our will to replace it with its own. [...] if securitizing actor „a‟ on behalf of community „A‟‟ claims „A‟‟ is threatened by „B‟‟, he or she will present „B‟ as an actor, as responsible for the threat, as an agent who had a choice.[50]" (Buzan 1998:44) Such a presumption on behalf of the functional actor/securitizer can be a predictor of intergroup anxiety because of the anticipation of negative actions, which causes the group to be seeing the other in a polarized image. According to a survey conducted in 2001, about 72% Israeli prefer living in a state without any Arabs whom they perceive as dangerous and fear them because of their readiness for suicide bombings, which heightens their fear to such a dimension that it penetrates the whole Israeli society. (Hass 2009:9) This assumption is likewise a source of intense hostility in intergroup attitudes, of marked discrimination in intergroup behavior, especially since the competition between the securitization actors is a "conflict of interests" out of the independent desires of the two for the referent object, they cannot simultaneously possess, and which is a token of the functional actor‟s identity. (Tajfel 1974:86,97)

Korostelina explains the polarization and the hostility in the relation to the threat actor in the securitizing move by employing the salience of the group/referent object, which influences the intergroup interactions, with high impact on conflict behavior and conflict readiness. She (Korostelina 2007:95) conducted several studies on the identity salience and the perception of the out-group, and found the following: the people with salient identity reflect negatively the out-groups, emphasizing the situations of insult in public places, using often generalizations and connecting negative emotional conditions with the out-group like rejection, antagonism, intensity, the out-group being attributed anger and disgust. These items are present especially in discourse, being employed also in the construction of the securitizing move, and inducing that the salience of the referent object and of the in-group can activate the intense aversion, which precede the securitizing act. The non-salient groups have mixed perceptions of the out-group, emphasizing the existence of both, positive and negative acts and attitudes in the interaction with the out-group, lacking the intensity and the mobilizing inner force of the salient groups for which the out-group expresses much malevolence.

Under these circumstances, the functional actor can be defined in terms of rivalry in relation to the threat actor. According to Sherif, a rival is someone who threatens with a sort of deprivation (of scarce resources), so that the deprived (affected) one is apt to meet him with antipathy and hostility, which is much more intense as the „rival" is considered to be a member of the out-group. Brown opines that the levels of antipathy towards the out-group increase direct proportional with the degree of threat to identity. (Brown in Tajfel 1982:161) Sherif argues that not even „hatred" is an exaggerated word. In case of rivalry, "when a group"s action for positive distinctiveness is

---

[50] This does not necessarily mean that countersecuritization is performed by the other part.

frustrated, impeded or in any way actively prevented by an out-group, this will (be pressured to fight for it) promote overt conflict and the hostility between the groups". (Worchel 1986:23) Given being these conditions, the relationship between the interests of the two actors has the potential to delineate their attitudinal relationship. (Tajfel 1974:81)

The rivalry between the functional actor and the threat actor may exhibit that behind inter-group behavior is self-esteem and motivation, the achievement or maintenance of power over an out-group in itself being a source of self-esteem, (Abrams 1990:45) this making at times the competition a necessary process[51]. Groups compete not only for resources, but for everything that can enhance their self-esteem, whereas those with a high self-esteem are generally more prone to engage in and create competition. (Kagan/Knight 1979:465) Should in their case self-esteem be depressed or threatened, the attitude of those affected may well be that of intergroup discrimination, which is one of many possible behavioral strategies to achieve it, this having a motivating force in intergroup behavior. (Abrams 1990:30,33,44) According to Korostelina (2007:69) "if the self-esteem is the most significant function of national identity any threat to the self-respect of a national group can inflame the readiness for conflict behavior." The influences are reflected also on the in-group where consistency becomes increasingly important when the self becomes implicated, this being a joining of forces for obtaining self-esteem, and a source of self-esteem as well. Thus, "competitive behavior between groups, at least in our culture, is extraordinarily easy to trigger off." (Tajfel in Worchel 1986:15)

This context may accordingly determine the functional actor to see itself the defender, the victim and the less responsible of the conflict escalation, which excuses for it the (extraordinary) actions that it takes (elimination of dissonance), for the other is „the prime mover". Seeing the other as responsible for the suffering leaves the functional actor no other viable alternative than the conflict and causes it to respond with

a.) vigilant (social) information processing about the nature of the threat;
b.) dysphonic rumination;
c.) sinister attribution error, that is to the malevolent reasons of the others;
d.) Biased punctuation of interaction history. (Kramer in Schopler 1998:247), which facilitates the securitizing act.

i.e. The study conducted by Hass (2009:15), asserts that "the more violent the environment is, the more likely it is that the media focus on the reporting about the own victims and therefore automatically blame the "others" for the harm to the own people." Thus, "maybe because of the

---

[51] Kagan and Knight opine the relation self esteem – competition is partially cultural dependent. (Kagan/Knight 1979:463)

Holocaust, for many Israelis, survival is above everything and justifies everything. [...] Because of the Holocaust on the one hand and suicide bombers on the other, most Israelis are willing to sacrifice basic human rights and to cross every red line in order to achieve security and survival" (Pogrund 2003:75 quoted in Hass 2009:17).

The above mentioned phenomena, enhances not only hostility exists between the two actors, but also prejudice and stereotypes, all being the consequences of (self-) categorization and comparison through which persons are defined by being systematically included or excluded from categories of „we" and „them", while being stated what they are or are not, in terms of common or criterial attributes of the respective categories[52]. (Tajfel 1982b:18,26) Tajfel asserts that the more the extreme the situation becomes "the more they will tend to treat members of the out-group as undifferentiated items in a unified social category, rather then in terms of their individual characteristics"[53]. (Tajfel in Worchel 1986:11) I.e. during the Second Intifada the Israeli government stated that all the suicide bombers came from the West Bank, causing the Palestinians from the West Bank to be regarded as a vital threat to Israel without distinguishing between suicide bombers and non-violent Palestinians, realizing thus a collective securitization. (Hass 2009:12) According to Stephan "conflict or threat generates prejudice regardless of whether or not there is an actual threat" (Stephan 2002:191,192), but if there is a threat, stereotypes and attitudes become more negative and extreme to avoid dissonance. (Korostelina 2007: 132) I.e. the Israeli fear the Palestinians, whom they regard either as terrorists or as future fundamentalists; the Palestinian see Israelis as settlers or soldiers. The stereotypes are on both sides, since they know each other only from media reporting, the territories being completely separated (Schenker 2008 in Hass 2009:17), but these are used in order to protect the own self-image. The felt threat, together with negative stereotypes – based on the social categorization processes by which the functional actor perceives himself as being superior, and manifests discriminatory attitudes in favor of his own group (Turner 2005:267) may cause the rise of prejudice (Stephan 2002:194) and discrediting, which, according to Sherif, is subsequently nourished by selective thinking that confirms his suppositions and interpretative tendencies. Once formed, the attitudes demand that the individual react in the characteristic way to these or related situations, persons, or groups (Sherif presented by Herkner 202), which does not have much to do with the reality of the threat actor since individuals and groups are seldom impartial in attitudes and reactions, which are inferred from the characteristic, selective nature of reaction"s situations.

---

[52] In social identification and categorization, this process is termed meta-contrast principle after Turner et al, 1987. this principle allows the perceiver to judge whether the intergroup differences are higher than the intra-group ones. This has a structuring function, as it helps the perceiver to see his environment in terms of meaningful, differentiated units. (Worchel 1998:127,128)
[53] The idea is not extrinsic to Freud which says that „by joining a group, a person acquires characteristics that are fundamentally different from those of an isolated individual."

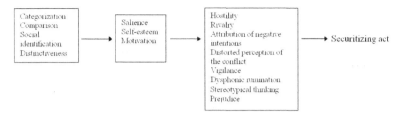

2.5 Why and when is there a Securitizing Act? The Balance Theory Confirmed by SIT

The relationship between the two actors and the attitudes of the functional actor towards the threat actor, that facilitate the securitizing act could be reflected by the collective axiology proposed by Korostelina and Rothbart (Identity, Morality and Threat, 2006), which dynamics is characterized by the degree of collective generality and the degree of axiological balance. *The collective generality* "refers to the ways in which in-group members categorize the other, how they simplify, or not, their defining character". This includes 4 characteristics: homogeneity of perceptions, long-term stability of beliefs, and resistance to change, the scope or range of the out-group. A high level of collective generality means seeing the out-group homogenous, demonstrating fixed patterns of conduct, etc. A low level of collective generality means a perception of the out-group as differentiated, ready for transformation, exhibiting various kinds of behavior, etc (Korostelina 2007:88) *The axiological balance* means a parallelism of virtues and vices of both groups. It helps identifying the morality, immorality, decency and cruelty in conduct of both parts. A high degree of axiological balance reflects the acknowledgment of virtues and vices, faults and failings of both groups, by the in-group, while a low degree of axiological balance reflects the perception of the in-group as superior and pure, while the out-group is evil. (Korostelina 2007:89)

Their combination results in 4 quadrants: *Quadrant 1* means *low axiological balance and high collective generality*, and is typical to protracted conflicts, where the out-group is portrayed as evil, cruel and its good parts are overshadowed by negative features, whereas the in-group is positive, virtuous and moral. Ethnicists would classify in this quadrant, since they support the rights of one part only and have a discourse of victimization of one"s community without reference to the suffering of the other. The evilness of the other part is nonetheless implicitly in such cases. *Quadrant 2* means *low axiological balance and low collective generality* and is typical to social classes. The in-group is pure and glorified, while the out-group has mixed values and virtues, the different „good" and „bad" voices being acknowledged. *Quadrant 3* means *high axiological balance and high collective generality*, and is typical to rigid stereotypes of interracial and gender discrimination. Both groups are seen as having positive and negative values. Out-groups are homogenous. *Quadrant 4 means high axiological balance and low collective generality*, and is typical to humanistic movements, peacemakers, human rights advocates, etc. Both groups are seen as having positive and negative values, yet the group salience and loyalty play a crucial part. (Korostelina 2007:90-91)

The figure exemplifies the state of the actors at the moment of a successful securitizing move (quadrant 1) and in the phase when the referent object is only politicized (quadrant 2). It

90   SOCIAL IDENTITY AND CONFLICT

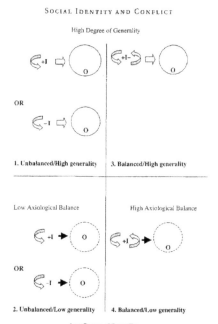

exemplifies how the security situation has probability to improve in the quadrant 2, where the threat actor is given a chance, by the mixed image the functional actor has about it, the securitizing act being avoidable, and displays wherefore it worsens in the case of quadrant 1, where the salient mobilized identity strengthens its perception of the out-group as a homogenous evil, eluding all possible cooperation (including power sharing) (Korostelina 2007:142) Likewise, the transition of quadrant 2 to quadrant 1 reflects the transition from politicization to securitization, where the securitizing act becomes a necessity.

The assumption that the discriminatory, prejudicial, conflictive and destructive relation between the two actors would not be positively solved from the perspective of the securitizing and functional actors, until the referent object is securely in the possession of the functional actor is supported also by the information provided by the securitization theory, and partly also by

Allport"s contact conditions meant to improve the intergroup relations. He assesses that there are 4 conditions for intergroup contact to reduce prejudice, of which the actors fulfill only a part in the securitization situation.

a.) *Equal group status* in the situation - there can be made only relative affirmations about the group status;

b.) *support of authorities*, law or custom - no exact affirmation can be made in this issue, yet, according to Tajfel (1974:80) the cutting fight for the preservation of the referent object may contain "the seeds of a secondary conflict of values: an intensification of discriminatory behavior and of hostile attitudes following upon the security threat may clash with generally accepted values representing the "official" ideology of a society". As long as the internal clash is solved in favor of the moderate block, the state does not support the conflict. But likewise can the state support a discriminative policy, that nourishes the in-group"s entitlement to the referent object;

c.) *common goals* - the two parts fail to have them, as described in the negative dependence, where they possess together the referent object without harming the functional actor;

d.) *Intergroup cooperation* – is not given. As long as the parts compete against the other to achieve the referent object, there cannot be the question about cooperation. Moreover, as long as the high self-esteem is threatened, the chances for cooperation go down.

Thus the dichotomous block securitizer/functional actor ←→ threat actor reflected by Heider"s balance triangle can be found again in Korostelina and Rothbart"s collective axiology, after the passage through SIT, whereas the severity of the antagonism is clearer due to the particularization of the generalized „negative attitudes" of Heider"s cycles.

3. Critique on the Limits of SIT in Clarifying the Functional Actor

The critique to the analysis of the securitization theory through the eyes of SIT could be separated on two levels: the substance level and the structure level. Regarding the *substance level*, with none of the two adopted auxiliary theories can it be explained whether the conflict around the referent object is regarded by all involved actors as an identity related issue, or for the securitizer or the threat actor the referent object is just an interest based item. It cannot be identified whether for the threat actor the referent object is reason for competition and for the other a reason for confrontation, or for both blocks it is about confrontation or counteraction.[54] Within the securitizing block no statements can be made whether the securitizer really shares the same belief as the functional actor, or just uses social identity of the functional actor to increase the group"'s loyalty and readiness for engagement, feigning a shared fate, a common deprivation, and thus a common interest. It cannot be said with certainty whether the securitizer involves the functional actor in the securitizing act because of other intentions in which the threat to the referent object

represents only the means to achieve its own interest. In like manner it cannot be differentiated whether the securitizer is itself a marionette of other interested actors or not, i.e. media, that can be regarded as "an element of civil society or it can be viewed as an instrument of the institutions of civil society including NGOs", becoming a power-penetrated area, like in Israel, where many politicians previously worked as editors - Zalman Shazar, former third President of Israel, former editor of Davar (Price 2004:119 in Hass 2009:5, Peri 2004: 1f in Hass 2009:14). Likewise, by SIT it cannot be explained if there is a security dilemma between the securitizer and the functional actor. For this reason, the severity and the duration of actions ad reactions of the actors cannot be evaluated.

By means of the 4 processes of SIT it cannot be generally estimated in a securitization situation, when or if there are changes in the intensity of the group/object salience, which is important in cases of semi-institutionalized or non-institutionalized „securitizing relations" since there are also other important variables. Among these are: in-group support, the willingness to fight, third out-group support and mediators, history of the relations, a special category with competence in the fight, etc. i.e. in the case of the average Israeli, the conflict with the Palestinians is very distant, mainly the soldiers reservists, settlers and peace activists and politicians, being directly engaged, these comprising all together less than 10 percent of the Israeli population. (Hass 2009:8)

---

[54] Korostelina proposes a 4 C Model of Identity based conflict: *Comparison* (We-They perception and favorable in-group comparison); *Competition* (instrumental conflicts of interest arise among counterpoised interactive groups that share or have the intention to share resources or power); *Confrontation* (the increase and ideologization of social one group"'s identity, transformation of conflict of interest into moral confrontation between the virtuous Us and the demonized Other; severe polarization of groups); *Counteraction* (discrimination, violence, genocide)". (Korostelina 2007:147)

SIT does not explain clearly how far securitization has chances of success, where the group boundaries are easily permeable, even in the case the referent object is an identity related issue, and to what degree and for how long is the functional actor disposed to engage in securitizing acts, and to reject desecuritization policies or leave them without consequences, i.e. in the case of multiple identities in multicultural environments.

Regarding the *structure level*, the dichotomous approach of SIT, as well as the social balance theory is not very efficient when trying to analyze the functional actor from the in-group and inter-group processes. The intergroup processes do not reveal so much the features of the functional actor that facilitate securitization but rather the consequences of the in-group processes, that become obvious due to the securitizing move and to its confrontation with the threat perspective. In this respect the dichotomous presentation of the function actor, based on the antagonism-structure of SIT is not the most proficient one, as it could be comprised in a more complex in-group processes approach.

Furthermore, the dichotomous perception of the security environment in which the blame for the security threat is put on „the others", which necessarily have to be removed, represents a deficit that cannot be covered not even by SIT, since the creativity option is categorically refused as a solution, when it should be taken into consideration. Both theories ignore the fact that issues from outside the group turn into threats in the context in which there are already vulnerabilities inside the group – and they are not created *loco* through the threat. In this case, the solution to the problem presupposes not so much the aggressive orientation towards the source of threat, which has to be eliminated in the first instance, as the securitization theory proposes, but rather an orientation towards the inside condition with the policy of vulnerability-reduction and removal of the real cause of danger. Only this could annul the threat, and avoid the legitimization of intolerance, radicality and exclusivism, that the actions emerging from both theories tend to achieve. To turn against the threat actor would otherwise mean the further weakening of the in-group by the „social competition" in an affected state, and the prolongation of the „disadvantageous" state of the in-group. If the launching of the securitization act is a necessity, it should than comprise a simultaneous fight on 2 fronts: one fight against the threat actor and one fight to remove the vulnerability.

Last but not least, SIT cannot be used extensively with low status groups in the case of securitization actors" analysis, because low stats groups usually seek changes by mobility or manifest abandon, out of lack of sufficient possibilities to fight with. This causes the securitization actors analysis through the SIT lenses to be partly biased in the direction of high status groups.

Conclusion

By the potential of SIT to tackle cognitive and motivational determinants of actors in the securitization theory, the two approaches prove to be complementary, even if the first is a psychological and the latter a security theory. SIT offers the possibility to gain an understanding in Buzan''s question on the internal conditions under which securitization is likely to occur (see Buzan 1998:32). Likewise, it succeeds in establishing a clear actors relations'' constellation. Nonetheless, as the critique to the theory''s potential has reflected, it does not cover the entire conflict spectrum of the securitization phenomenon, since the latter comprises much more than a social psychological calculus (internal motivations), which serves especially there where the general context is not yet evident and the actors are not yet (clearly) established. In order to understand what external motives facilitate the consent to the securitizing move it is fundamental to consider also the social political, cultural, or historical aspects in which occurs the securitizing move.

Even if SIT is comprehensive in explaining the features of the functional actor, this theoretical approach is not the only one possible. The social psychological theory is mainly there primordial, where the social construct bases on a collectivist apprehension of the environment, for in the rationalist-individual ones, the self-serving materialistic strategies entail decisions and actions. An alternative (or a supplement) may as well be represented by the theories concerning intergroup relations and behavior focused on deprivation. The difference between these theories lies not in the principle, but in the emphasis they lay and the perspectives they offer. The *realistic group theory* developed by Muzafer Sherif in 1967, affirms that "real conflict of group interests causes intergroup conflicts" (Sherif quoted by Worchel 1986:7), and puts forward insights that are not rejected by SIT. The *relative deprivation theory* developed by Stouffer (1949) and continued by Runciman and Gurr (1970), explains the conditions under which deprivation is likely to appear and addresses the consequences of deprivation on subsequent individual participation in collective actions. This theory tackles the individual''s protests under the conditions of its strong sense of personal control over the situation, where intergroup inequalities are not as frustrating as the intra-group inequalities. (Berkowitz in Hogg 1988:38, Hogg 1988:42)

Nonetheless, adopting the social psychological approach, the actors and objects left completely open in the securitization theory become more sedimented, making securitization to a certain degree predicable. (Williams 2003:514) The social psychological dimension explains how the intense relation of the actors with their surroundings has the power to turn an issue political, and thus „securitizable", as according to Schmitt, "every religious, moral, economic, ethical, or other antithesis transforms itself into a political one if it is sufficiently strong to group human beings according to friend and enemy". (quoted by Williams 2003:516) To this extent it emphasizes, that the key to a successful securitization stays not only with the intrinsic nature of the referent object, nor with the specific threat rhetoric, as the fathers of the securitization theory assert, but also with the type of the actors"relation to their environment (Williams 2003:516) and in like manner with the characteristics of the audience itself[55]. These aspects, which are most clearly probably in the case of societal security, where the referent object is the identity of a group itself, remained underdeveloped in the securitization theory. To this extent, when considering the classification of the actors according to the degree of institutionalization, a further differentiation of the types of institutions and an analysis of their characteristics would also be helpful.

SIT reflects that the relationship of the functional actor with its environment evolves simultaneously with the development and the consolidation of its social identity, each action and reaction contributing to the development of the two, and both influencing each other. To this extent, it emphasizes that the securitizing move falls on a ground that has already started to shape, and that the consent to the securitizing act comes as a reaction of the already achieved stage of identity development: a strong identification with the group that offers a high/strong identity, this group being/becoming very salient for the functional actor, and determining it to manifest loyalty, responsibility, decisiveness, dynamism, receptivity, etc for the referent object, which is for him a source of pride, satisfaction, self-esteem, legitimacy, and much more than that. In the securitization process its attitudes and values are so strong that they make the functional actor prone to aggressiveness or conflict readiness, and create a stereotypical, biased perception of itself and the opponent, who in the functional actor"s distorted judgment is not less than a hostile rival with negative intensions. This causes the functional actor to react with vigilance, dysphonic rumination, intolerance of the new situation and blindness to other solutions than the direct conflict, and much more than that.

In this context, it remains a question to answer how this evolution is prepared intentionally by the environment to the purpose of obtaining the consent to the securitizing act. As a mere example could be mentioned how the very dynamical media landscape with its tremendous visual impact influences the functional actor"s identity construct, the determination of its position and thus its security information assimilation, preparing a fertile ground for the securitizing move. This poses a challenge to the securitization theory because in comparison to the institutionalized, official state representatives, the media has a more dynamic power and capacity to change the

---

[55] I.e. there is the sovereignty of the functional actor that crowns its relation to its environment. Schmitt concludes "Sovereign is he who decides upon the exception" and "whether there is to be an extreme emergency as well as what must be done to eliminate it. Although he stands outside the normally valid legal system, he nevertheless belongs to it, for it is he who must decide whether the constitution needs to be suspended in its entirety" (1996:5-7)

polarization degree in the securitization constellation, offering the functional actor another awareness of its „sovereignty". Together with the inclusion of the social identity scale, this would represent another dimension of discourse analysis. Likewise it does bring into discussion the manner of consenting to the securitizing act. (verbal, non-verbal, internal…)

References

Abrams, Dominic/Michael A. Hogg (ed.) (1990): Social Identity Theory. Constructive and Critical Advances. Harvester Wheatsheaf, Hempstead.

Brown, Ruppert (2000):Group Processes. 2nd ed. Blackwell Publishers. Oxford

Buzan, Barry (1983/1991): People, States and Fear: An Agenda for International Security Studies in the Post-cold War Era, New York: Harvester.

Buzan, Barry/Ole Wæver (1997): Slippery? Contradictory? Sociologically untenable? The Copenhagen School Replies. In: Review of International Studies. Cambridge University Press, Vol. 23, Issue 02, p. 241-250.

Buzan, Barry/Ole Wæver/Jaap de Wilde (1998): Security: A New Framework for Analysis. London u.a.: Rienner.

Demetriou, Olga/Ayla Gürel (2008): Human Rights, Civil Society and Conflict in Cyprus: Exploring the Relationships. Case Study Report, SHUR wp 03/08, International Peace Research Institute, Oslo (PRIO) Cyprus Centre. El.ed. accessed 20.02.2009 www.luiss.it/shur

Dovidio, John F./Peter Glick/ Laurie A. Budman: On the Nature of Prejudice. Fifty years after Allport. Blackwell Publishing USA.

Durkheim, Emile (1895): The rules of the sociological method. Chpt.5. Rules for the Explanation of Social Facts Tr. by W.D. Halls. New York: The Free Press. el. ed. Accessed 15.12.2008 http://varenne.tc.columbia.edu/bib/texts/durkheim_rules_chap5.html

Ellemers, Naomi (2002): Social Identity and Relative Deprivation. In: Walker, Iain (Ed) Relative Deprivation. Specification, Development, and Integration. Cambridge University Press.

Emmers, Ralf (2007): Securitization. In: Contemporary Security Studies. Alan Collins. Oxford University Press.

Grayson, Kyle (2003): Securitization and the Boomerang Debate: A Rejoinder to Liotta and Smith-Windsor. In: Security Dialogue 2003; 34; 337, DOI: 10.1177/ 09670106030343009. el. ed. Accessed 11.02.09 http://sdi.sagepub.com/cgi/reprint/34/3/337

Gromes, Thorsten/Thorsten Bonacker (2007): The Concept of Securitisation as a Tool for Analysing the Role of Human-Rights-Related Civil Society in Ethno-Political Conflicts. University of Marburg SHUR wp 05/07 March 2007.el.ed. accessed 12.11.08 www.luiss.it/shur

Hass, Rabea (2009): Media as Civil Society Actors in Israel and their Influence on the Israel-Palestine Conflict, Marburg University, SHUR wp 01/09, Feb. 2009. el. Ed. Accessed 25.02.09 www.luiss.it/shur

Heider, Fritz (1959): The Psychology of Interpersonal Relations. John Wiley & Sons, Inc. NY.

Herkner, Werner (1991): Lehrbuch Sozialpsychologie. 5.Auflage. Verlag Hans Huber, Bern, Stuttgart, Toronto.

Hogg A. Michael/Dominic Abrams (1988): Social Identifications. A Social Psychology of Intergroup Relations and Group Processes. Routledge. London, NY.

Hogg A. Michael/Deborah Terry (ed.) (2001): Social Identity Processes in Organisational Context. Psychology Press. Philadelphia.

Homans, George Caspar (1974): Social Behavior. Its Elementary Forms. Revised Ed. Harcourt Brace Jovanovich, Inc. Harvard University.

Jost, John/Roderick Kramer (2002): The System Justification Motive in Intergroup Relations. In: Mackie, Diane/Eliot R. Smith (ed): From Prejudice to Intergroup Emotions. Differentiated Reactions to Social Groups. Psychology Press. NY and Hove.

Kagan, Spencer/George P. Knight (1979): Cooperation-Competition and Self-Esteem: A Case of Cultural Relativism. In: Journal of Cross-Cultural Psychology; 10; 457 DOI: 10.1177/0022022 179104004, el. ed. accessed 09.02.09 http://jcc.sagepub.com/cgi/content/abstract/10/4/457

Korostelina Karina V. (2007): Social Identity and Conflict. Structures, Dynamics, and Implications. Palgrave Macmillan. NY

Levine, Mark/ Clare Cassidy, Gemma Brazier, Stephen Reicher: Self-categorization and bystander non-intervention: Two experimental studies. Lancaster University, Lancaster/ St Andrew's University, St Andrew's. (research supported by Economic and Social Research Council Grant 1133 25 1054 under its Violence Research Programme). El ed. Accessed 10.02.2009 www.psych.lancs.ac.uk/people/uploads/MarkLevine20050211T141936.pdf

McDonald, Matt (2008): Securitization and the Construction of Security. In: European Journal of International Relations, vol. 14: p. 563 - 587. DOI: 10.1177/1354066108097553. El ed. Accessed 10.02.2009 http://ejt.sagepub.com/cgi/reprint/14/4/563

Mummendey, Amelie (199): Positive distinctiveness and social discrimination: an old couple living in divorce. In: European Journal of Social Psychology, Vol. 25/1995, 657-670.el. ed. Accessed 06.02.09 http://www3.interscience.wiley.com/cgi-bin/fulltext/112464324/PDFSTART

Roe, Paul (2008): Actor, Audience(s) and Emergency Measures: Securitization and the UK's Decision to Invade Iraq. In: Security Dialogue 2008; 39; 615, DOI: 10.1177/ 0967010608098212. El. ed. Accessed 11.02.09 http://sdi.sagepub.com/cgi/content/abstract/39/6/615

Schopler, John/Chester Insko (Ed.) (1998): Intergroup Cognition and Intergroup Behavior. Lawrence Erlbaum Associates, Mahwah, New Jersey.

Sherif, Muzafer (1948): An Outline of Social Psychology. Harper&Brothers Publishers, N.Y.

Schmitt, Carl (1996): Politische Theologie : vier Kapitel zur Lehre von der Souveränität. 7. Aufl. Duncker & Humblot, Berlin.

Schneider, Wolfgang Ludwig (2008): Grundlagen der soziologischen Theorie. Kapitel 2. Das Problem sozialer Ordnung und das normativistische Modell des Handelns: Talcott Parsons 3. Auflage, VS Verlag fuer Sozialwissenschaften

Spears, Russell/Bertjan Doosje/Naomi Ellemers (1997): Self-Stereotyping in the Face of Threats to Group Status and Distinctiveness: The Role of Group Identification. In: Personality and Social Psychology Bulletin 1997; 23; 538 DOI: 10.1177/0146167297235009. el ed. Accessed 07.02.2009 http://psp.sagepub.com/cgi/reprint/23/5/538

Stephan, Walter/Lausanne Renford (2002): The Role of Threat in Intergroup Relations. In: Mackie, Diane/Eliot R. Smith (ed): From Prejudice to Intergroup Emotions. Differentiated Reactions to Social Groups. Psychology Press. NY and Hove.

Tajfel, Henri (1974): Social identity and intergroup behavior. Trends and Developments.In: Social Science Information 1974; 13; 65-93, DOI: 10.1177/053901847401300204. el. ed. Accessed 26.01.2009 http://ssi.sagepub.com/cgi/reprint/13/2/65

Tajfel, Henri (1982/a): Gruppenkonflikt und Vorurteil. Entstehung und Funktion sozialer Stereotypen. Kapitel 5: Soziale Kategorisierung, soziale Idenitität und sozialer Vergleich. Verlag Hans Huber. Bern, Stuttgart, Wien.

Tajfel, Henri (1982/b): Social Identity and Intergroup Relations. Cambridge University Press.

Tajfel, Henri (1984): The social dimension. European developments in social psychology. Cambridge University Press.

Taylor, Donald M./Fathali M Moghaddam (1994):Theories of Intergroup Relations. International Social Psychological Perspectives. 2nd Edition. Praeger. Westport, Connecticut, London.

Turner, John/Katherine Reynolds (2005): The Social Identity in Intergroup Relations: Theories, Themes, and Controversies. In: Brewer, Marilynn?Miles Hewstone (2005): Self and Social Identity. Blackwell Publishing. Oxford.

Tyler R. Tom/Steven L. Blader (2000): Cooperation in Groups. Procedural Justice, Social Identity and Behavioral Engagement. Psychology Press. Philadelphia.

Viehöver, Willy/Thomas Kern (2002): Kritische Theorie als Theorie des kommunikativen Handelns - Jürgen Habermas. In: Stark, Carsten/ Christian Lahausen (Hrsg.): Theorien der Gesellschaft. Oldenbourg Verlag München Wien.

Wagner, Ulrich/Jost Stellmacher (2000): Gruppenprozesse. Kurseinheit: Intergruppenprozesse. Fernuniversitaet Hagen.

Williams, Michael C. (2003):Words, Images, Enemies: Securitization and International Politics. In: International Studies Quarterly (2003) 47, 511–531. el. Ed. Accessed 22.02.2009 http://www3.interscience.wiley.com/cgi-bin/fulltext/118869079/PDFSTART

Worchel, Stephen/Austin William G. (1986): Psychology of Intergroup Relations. 2nd ed. Nelson-Hall Publishers Chicago.

Worchel, Stephen/Francisco Morales, Dario Paez, Jean Claude Deschamps (1998): Social Identity. International Perspectives. Sage Publications Ltd. London.

Zick, Andreas (2008): Die Konflikttheorie der Theorie sozialer Identität. In: Bonacker, Thorsten (Hrsg.) (2008): Sozialwissenschaftliche Konflikttheorien. Eine Einfuehrung. 4. Auflage. VS Verlag fuer Sozialwissenschaften. Wiesbaden.